T0285281

# IMPACT

# REDEFINED

# IMPACT

# REDEFINED

## NICK

## LYNCH

Transforming Partnerships, Social Moments, and
Personal Connections to Drive Change

WILEY

For general information on our other products and services or for technical support, please contact
our Customer Care Department within the United States at (800) 762-2974, outside the United States
at (317) 572-3993 or fax (317) 572-4002.

Wiley also publishes its books in a variety of electronic formats. Some content that appears in print
may not be available in electronic formats. For more information about Wiley products, visit our web
site at www.wiley.com.

*Library of Congress Cataloging-in-Publication Data is Available:*

ISBN 9781394237098 (Cloth)
ISBN 9781394237104 (ePub)
ISBN 9781394237111 (ePDF)

Cover Image and Design: Basic Consultants, Inc.

SKY10069782_031524

*This book is dedicated to the amazing nonprofits and the passionate individuals steering the ship whose unwavering commitment to driving social impact forward and making a real difference in the world inspires us all. Your tireless efforts illuminate the path toward a brighter future for us all.*

# Contents

# Acknowledgments

As I reflect on the incredible journey of creating this book, my heart is filled with profound gratitude for the unwavering love and support that has surrounded me. Writing a book has been a goal of mine for a very long time, and I want to express my deepest appreciation to those who have been instrumental in making it possible.

First and foremost, I want to extend my heartfelt gratitude to my wife, Joslin, and my son, Noah, who have been my unwavering pillars of support and constant sources of inspiration. Your love, patience, and encouragement have been the driving force behind this project, and I am profoundly grateful for the beautiful moments we've shared throughout this journey.

To my parents, your love and support have been a guiding light in my life, especially during the challenging days of my early battle with cancer. Your infinite belief in me has fueled my determination to create positive change in the world.

I also want to express my heartfelt thanks to the Make-A-Wish Foundation for profoundly changing the trajectory of my life when they granted my wish to go to Disneyland. That experience was a turning point that instilled in me a deep sense of purpose and a commitment to making a difference in the lives of others.

To Wiley, thank you for taking a chance on a social impact enthusiast who is passionate about making the world a better place. Your belief in the importance of this work has been instrumental in bringing this book to fruition, and I am honored to be a part of the Wiley family.

To all the readers, I am deeply appreciative of your interest in the topics discussed in this book. Your dedication to creating positive social impact aligns with my vision, and I hope the insights within these pages inspire and empower you to continue making a lasting difference.

This book represents the culmination of the collective support, love, and inspiration I have received from these incredible individuals and organizations. Thank you for joining me on this meaningful journey and may our shared commitment to impact create waves of positive change that resonate far and wide.

With heartfelt appreciation,

Nick

# About the Author

**Nick Lynch** has spent his professional career building solutions for brands to better identify and target their audiences online. Nick is more than a businessman: from personal experience as a former Make-A-Wish recipient who survived cancer at an early age, Nick is passionate about nonprofit organizations. When the COVID-19 pandemic suddenly forced many nonprofits into the digital space, it triggered Nick to think strategically about solving the challenges of creating opportunities to thrive without in-person events. This prompted Nick into creating Collidescope, an innovative technology and services provider in the social impact space, dedicated to activating and empowering social change through cutting-edge digital solutions. Collidescope empowers global causes, influencers, and organizations to collaborate and measure their cumulative influence and impact, as well as companies looking to add or improve their corporate social responsibility initiatives. Out of 2,900-plus start-ups analyzed, StartUs named Collidescope as one of the top five Social Tech Startups to Watch in 2021.

After spending nearly two decades developing expertise in digital media and advertising technology for public media brands, high-growth private companies, and start-ups, Nick Lynch knows what truly drives revenue, performance, and innovation: execution. Leveraging his diversified product experience from MySpace to

Fox, the Rubicon Project, and Amobee has helped him build profitable products throughout his career. Nick has developed a unique expertise in marketing and advertising technology to enable companies to create a dynamic digital presence.

Nick has landed coverage in print and broadcast outlets around the world, including TechCrunch, Yahoo!, MediaPost, ClickZ, Adotas, Beet.TV, and Forbes.

# Introduction

The social impact landscape is dramatically shifting. The effect COVID-19 has had on the world, beyond the health implications, has changed the way individuals, corporations, and nonprofit organizations look at delivering impact. In most cases, it has accelerated the way corporations and organizations use new tools and technology to achieve impact. And though there is now more attention to and participation in social impact activities, there is also more distance and confusion about how organizations and corporations can build communities, increase long-term engagement, develop mutually beneficial partnerships, and amplify the amazing works they are undertaking. So how do we navigate this new world of partnerships, social media, and other gateways to social impact?

## The Power of a Wish

First, let me tell you a bit more about myself. After all, you may be wondering why it is that you should believe whatever this stranger is telling you! My name is Nick. When I was three, I was diagnosed with a stage 3 Wilms tumor in my right kidney. For months, my parents would take me to the doctor, where he would review my symptoms, my vitals, and my labs, and come up with the conclusion that nothing was wrong. When we would return home after every visit, my mom's intuition was telling her that there was something else going on. And after each mostly uneventful visit, that intuition grew stronger. Until she finally decided to get a second opinion from another doctor.

Within the first 15 minutes of meeting with our new doctor, he agreed with my mother, and that based on my lab results, I needed to go to the Oakland Children's Hospital emergency room immediately. By the time they found my cancer, it had spread from my right kidney, down to my groin, and into my inferior vena cava—the largest vein in the human body, which carries deoxygenated blood from the lower body to the heart. The operating report said that the tumor had "fingerlings" that were centimeters from my heart. After six hours of surgery, a few weeks of radiation, and months of chemotherapy, I was cancer free, and have been now for nearly 37 years.

At the tail end of my chemotherapy, a family friend had recommended me to a relatively new nonprofit out of Phoenix, Arizona, called the Make-A-Wish Foundation. Their organization granted "wishes" to children who were battling life-threatening illnesses. My wish was to go to Disneyland. The wish was filled with limousine rides to and from the airport, my first flight, multiple days at Disneyland, and, most important, memories that eclipsed the trauma of childhood cancer. Not just for me, but for my family, too. When I think about that time in my life, even though I was only three, I mostly only have memories of my wish and not the hospital stays and treatments.

Cancer can be a strange, common bond between people. I have yet to meet someone that hasn't directly or indirectly been affected by it. Typically, the idea of having cancer, surviving cancer, or knowing someone who has had or is battling cancer creates feelings of fear and despair. All totally understandable and rational feelings to have. My mom and dad are both cancer survivors as well, so I have been entrenched in the disease repeatedly throughout my life from multiple vantage points. But I view cancer differently. Yes, it is scary, but it's never been a better time to be fighting as modern medicine continuingly is finding new ways to treat and beat the disease. And so, we fight. It's this fight that has shaped my perspectives.

My cancer experience has been a source of pride and confidence for me. The scar down the middle of my chest has always reminded me that if I can survive cancer, I can do anything. I have used this to power through any challenge I've ever encountered in my life. I believe that using this experience in this way, has enabled me to be successful in my personal and professional life. And for the last 16-plus years, I have been able to build a successful marketing and advertising career that has been focused on building solutions for brands and advertisers to better target their audiences on digital and social media.

Eight years ago, my life came full circle. I had recently found out that my wife was pregnant with our son. I am sure every parent goes through that moment when things get real. And when I saw him for the first time on the ultrasound, things got *very* real. I was suddenly transported back to 1987, but in my parents' shoes, empathizing with them and what it's like to be a parent. Though there was nothing wrong with my son, I still began to feel their helplessness of not being able to do anything to heal their child, the agony of pacing in the waiting room while their son was being operated on, and also the immense joy of seeing their son in remission and eating ice cream under the fireworks-filled sky of Disneyland. Through this wave of emotion, I had an epiphany, and one thing became clear: it was time to do anything and everything I could to support Make-A-Wish. Over the last eight years, I have supported Make-A-Wish Greater Los Angeles through fundraising, developing their young professional's council, and providing leadership on their advisory board. I have used my professional expertise and network to guide and scale impact for this amazing organization. I have also become a volunteer wish granter, enabling me to conduct the full wish experience from discovery to reveal. After I granted my first wish, I sat in my car and cried. The emotion was overwhelming, and I knew that child whose wish I granted and his family's experience was going to change their life in the most meaningful and positive way.

## When Personal and Professional Collide

In late February 2020, I was on a business trip to Southeast Asia, which as we all remember was ground zero for COVID at that time. I foolishly underestimated its seriousness and flew out to meet clients. At the time, I was running a global influencer marketing company and was scheduled for my quarterly trip to the region. Though at that time, we were getting more and more information about COVID, its seriousness hadn't really contextualized for me until I landed in Hong Kong. A large international hub, usually shuffling more than 200,000 people in and out of Hong Kong per day, was completely empty. From my gate to the airport lounge in the international terminal was about a half-mile walk. During that walk I would have typically navigated around thousands of people. This time, I only saw seven other people. All of the shops were closed. Looking outside the windows at the tarmac I saw dozens of airplanes triple and quadruple parked in a surreal pattern of wings, tails, and cockpits. It was a scene out of an apocalyptic movie. As I made my way to my connecting flight to Singapore, I was imagining what the rest of my trip was going to look like. As you can imagine, it was filled with masked meetings and temperature checks at every stop. But it was during one of these masked meetings that sparked an idea that would change the course of my life, again.

On my last day in Singapore, I was meeting a friend who told me, "This is just the beginning. Things are going to get bad, people will lose their jobs, and we will all need help." He knew my background in advertising and influencer marketing and asked, "What can you do to help?" His tone, body language, and question stuck with me for the rest of my trip. And for the next 30 hours of travel time back home, all I could think about was what I could do. When I landed back in the states, I had a pitch deck, financial model, and name for an idea that would answer my friend's question: Collidescope.

The concept of Collidescope was the amalgamation of my personal and professional worlds—they were "colliding" . . . get it? I knew that brands were spending billions of dollars a year in cause marketing and corporate social responsibility and that they would spend more directly with mission-driven organizations if there was better insights and transparency into not only how those dollars made an impact but also if the business saw any meaningful and positive lift. I also knew that influencers were becoming a fast-growing and legitimate marketing channel, and these influencers would happily use their platform to promote vision and value-aligned missions if they were presented with opportunities to do so. It was this triangulation of brands, non-profits, and influencer stakeholders that was the start of Collidescope. I built some tools, technology, and processes that helped identify corporate partners, nonprofits, and influencers that had value alignment, facilitated these collaborations, and measured the efficacy of these partnerships. We coined the phrase *Double ROI*, which is a term we use to describe how we measure return on investment for the corporate partner in terms of business benefits and return on impact in terms of mission benefits. By looking at this holistically and identifying correlations between tactics and outcomes, stakeholders are able to understand the value of their participation in the impact equation.

Our first campaigns were in partnership with our friends in Singapore, where we powered a social enterprise called We The Good. Through this partnership we were able to create hundreds of social media posts with five influencer partners, which enabled our cause partners to reach more than 5 million people and generate nearly $150,000. We knew that this was the start of something special. Since then, we've been recognized as a top-five social start-up to watch, and our innovative products and processes have helped our clients raise millions of dollars and reach tens of millions of people. We are now commonly referred to as the *Deloitte For Social Good*.

## The Emergence of Three Key Elements

Over the last nearly four years of building and scaling our impact platform in Collidescope, and working with brands, nonprofits, and social media influencers to build collaborative partnerships at scale, I have started to notice interesting patterns emerge. Certain trends, when harnessed, bring about exponential impact and produce positive results.

Throughout my hands-on experience in the impact space, I have found that real, meaningful change is slow, old habits are hard to break, and even though new technologies emerge and evolve, adoption sometimes feels forced or, even worse, haphazardly implemented. In conversation after conversation and engagement after engagement with our Collidescope clients and partners, we could see the struggle and fear of change. COVID essentially forced every single nonprofit to become digital experts, almost overnight. Though some organizations have been innovative in their community-building and storytelling efforts, when it comes to their digital presence and use of tools, the vast majority of organizations weren't. As we worked to support this transition, it was obvious that leadership felt lost. We looked for ways to apply what they have always done to this new reality. But with all of this new noise, where do you start?

It is in this chaos that I found three simple truths, key elements that simplify process and purpose. These three key elements can be used, returned to, and reflected on to help start, rebuild, or refocus your social impact mission. Throughout this book, my goal is to share these elements with you to help achieve the impact you desire. Whether this is an impact in your local community, region, state, country, or something that you can apply to the global community, these elements apply to all scenarios. Before we examine these three elements more closely, let's take a broader look at businesses that are focusing on social impact with some success.

When businesses, nonprofits, and similar entities say that they focus on social impact, they are referring to the effects that their actions and decisions have on society. This can include positive and negative effects and can be related to a wide range of issues, such as the environment, the economy, and social and cultural issues. You can look to businesses like Ben and Jerry's, or recently, Patagonia, who both shocked the world and showed leadership by donating the entire companies' profits to charity.

Businesses that are focused on social impact often prioritize the well-being of society and the environment over short-term profit, and they may take actions such as investing in sustainable practices, supporting local communities, and promoting diversity and inclusion. What these businesses find is that by making these investments and executing on these initiatives, their margins increase, the employees are happier, are more engaged, and stay at the company longer, all while the value of their company increases. These businesses may also measure their social impact using specific metrics and key performance indicators, like the

United Nations 17 Sustainable Development Goals (commonly referred to as SDGs), to assess the extent to which they are achieving their social and environmental goals.

Social impact is a wide-ranging topic, one that can be difficult to discuss without losing focus. However, at its core, there are key areas that I have identified that provide a strong base for any social impact organization to start and grow from. This book has been broken down into three key parts—one for each of the three elements—to keep this discussion more efficient and focused:

- Element 1: Social
- Element 2: Partnerships
- Element 3: Human

These three elements are the pillars of the social, partnerships, human (SPH) model, my impact philosophy that I explain in depth throughout this entire book. The right mix of these three core elements are the ingredients for any person, team, or entire organization to being impactful, regardless of mission, size, region, or industry.

## Element 1: Social

First, we have the **social element**. On its surface, this may seem obvious. Everyone uses social media. It is integrated into everything that we do. And, yes, social media is a part of the social element, but there is so much more than just a social media presence. We are more connected than ever, and this is in large part due to social media. We are no longer limited by our geography or by the close-knit circle we have. On top of this, social media as a way to connect is evolving in itself—we are not only able to connect more easily but also algorithms and artificial intelligence (AI) are growing increasingly strong and making these connections even easier to make. Though we are more digitally connected than ever before, we have also never been more disconnected in real life. According to US Census Bureau surveys,[1] Americans have been spending less time with friends and more time alone than they did before the pandemic, which has only intensified the sense of social isolation. As we get back to "normal," get past the pandemic and lockdowns, how do we create real and meaningful connections outside of social media? How do you take what you've built on social media to the real world? As an impact organization, community building is key to enhancing growth and infusing real and digital social elements to build, reinforce, and empower your community, and it is vitally important to the evolution of how and where you tell your story.

At its core, the social element operates as a fundamental piece of modern existence. Although the term *social media* immediately comes to mind, the scope of the social element transcends mere digital interactions. Yes, social media forms an integral part, but it is merely a facet of the multidimensional spectrum that constitutes the essence of social connectivity. The resonance of the social element lies in its capacity to intertwine lives, transcend geographical boundaries, and revolutionize the dynamics of human relationships. This provides an epic opportunity to develop relationships that were previously hidden, unattainable, impossible to maintain, and to grow. Even us introverts crave some level of social engagement and interaction, and it has never been easier to develop and deliver these social experiences.

---

[1] https://www.pbs.org/newshour/show/why-americans-are-lonelier-and-its-effects-on-our-health

## The Web of Connectivity

The omnipresence of social media is a testament to the integration of the social element in our lives. However, its significance extends far beyond scrolling feeds and posting updates. The digital age has gifted humanity with unprecedented connectivity, shattering limitations imposed by distance and time zones. This has led to the weaving of intricate webs of interconnectedness that span the globe. The traditional confines of geographical location and limited social circles are no longer restrictive barriers. When harnessed and blended with in-person social engagement, it provides a potent recipe for community activation, building, and ultimately amplifying impact.

## The Evolution of Connection: Algorithms and AI

The very essence of connection is evolving in tandem with the rapid advancements of algorithms and AI. These technological marvels, fueled by data-driven insights, have amplified our ability to establish and strengthen connections. Algorithms facilitate the discovery of like-minded individuals and potential allies, effectively reducing the barriers to forming meaningful relationships. The integration of AI enhances the accuracy of matchmaking, enabling connections to be made with individuals who share common interests, values, and goals.

## Transitioning from Virtual to Real

Yet, a pivotal question emerges: How does one transform digital connections into tangible relationships that extend into the real world? The answer lies in the art of community building. The foundation of impact growth rests on the cultivation of communities that resonate on digital and physical planes. Infusing authentic social elements into these communities spurs their development, reinforcement, and empowerment. The interplay between virtual and real interactions forms an interconnected narrative that shapes how and where stories are told.

The demand for this interconnectedness is at an all-time high. We crave ways that what we discover digitally and implement physically, and the question of how to transform digital connections into tangible, real-world relationships is more pertinent than ever. The journey from virtual interaction to meaningful, physical connection requires a delicate blend of strategies and an appreciation for the art of community building. To truly harness the potential of digital platforms for personal and professional growth, we must focus on cultivating communities that resonate seamlessly in the digital and physical spaces.

The first step in this transformative process is to understand the pivotal role that communities play in our lives. Communities are not just groups of people with shared interests; they are the underlying threads of our societal tapestry. In the digital and social era, these communities have taken on new forms and structures, with social media platforms and online forums like Reddit serving as their virtual meeting places. However, the challenge lies in ensuring that these virtual communities evolve beyond the confines of computer code.

The interplay between virtual and real interactions is where the magic happens. Digital connections provide us with the initial platform to meet and engage with like-minded people, but it's the transition to real-world interactions that solidifies these connections. The beauty of this interplay is that it allows for a seamless flow of experiences and narratives between these two worlds.

Take, for example, a group of people who share a passion for environmental conservation. They might connect through online forums and social media, sharing ideas and resources virtually. However, it's when they come together for a tree-planting event or a beach cleanup that the true impact of their community is felt.

These real-world interactions not only strengthen their individual relationships but also enable them to build collective togetherness, while being able to make a tangible difference in the world, turning their shared passion into action. This is the exponential power of the combined digital and physical social element.

In this interconnected narrative of digital and physical interactions, stories are told and shared in ways that were previously unimaginable. Social media platforms, for instance, enable individuals to document their journeys and experiences, sharing them with a global audience. These stories inspire others to join communities, creating a wave of connection and empowerment.

But it's important to recognize that community building is not a one-size-fits-all. Different communities require tailored approaches and strategies. Some may thrive through in-person meetups, and others may find their strength in virtual gatherings. The key is to strike a balance that allows for seamless transitions between these two spaces.

## Community Building: The Impetus for Evolution

Community building is at the heart of harnessing the social element for transformative growth. The significance of vibrant and engaged communities cannot be emphasized enough, particularly when it comes to driving positive impact.

When we think about creating meaningful change in the world, we often look to communities as the driving force behind it. These communities serve as incubators for ideas, a space where shared aspirations take root and collective action gains momentum. Within these digital and physical spaces, individuals find not just like-minded peers but also a sense of belonging and shared purpose.

As we become a more digitally integrated society, the synergy between real-world gatherings and digital engagement is paramount.

As members of such communities engage both online and offline, they transcend the boundaries of screens and keyboards. The sense of togetherness, shared purpose, and the knowledge that they are part of something bigger than themselves empower individuals to take meaningful action. They become catalysts for change, extending their impact far beyond the confines of their digital worlds.

## Forging Connections in the Real World

Transitioning from virtual connections to real-world relationships is a process that requires deliberate and intentional efforts. Digital interactions can provide a valuable starting point for connecting with others, but the true depth of relationships often emerges through face-to-face meetings and shared experiences.

Physical meetups, workshops, seminars, and collaborative projects play a pivotal role in this journey. These events provide the opportunity for individuals who have connected online to come together in person. In these real-world settings, people can engage in meaningful conversations, share experiences, and work toward common goals. It is within these instances that digital familiarity can transform into deeper, more meaningful bonds.

Face-to-face interactions have a unique power to humanize our connections. Because of social media, it's easy to forget that there are real people behind the screens. Meeting someone in person breaks down the barriers that can exist online and enables individuals to see each other as whole, complex beings. This personal connection fosters a sense of trust and mutual understanding that can be challenging to achieve virtually.

Collaborative projects and shared experiences during physical meetups often lead to a sense of accomplishment and shared achievement. When individuals work together to achieve a common goal, whether it's a community service project, a creative project, or a professional initiative, they create lasting bonds. These shared accomplishments become part of the story that the community tells about itself, reinforcing the sense of belonging and shared purpose.

The harmonious convergence of virtual and real-world interactions is where the true authenticity of the social element shines. When digital connections translate into real-world relationships, the narratives shared within the community gain credibility and depth. The stories become more than just words on a screen; they become living, breathing experiences that shape the collective identity of the community.

## The Power of Narrative in Social Change

The power of storytelling is nothing short of transformative. Stories have a unique ability to enhance and bind our alignment, touching hearts and minds, and inspiring action. The social element explores the impact of storytelling, illuminating how it connects individuals to the missions of mission-driven organizations and amplifies the voices of those striving to make a difference.

At its core, storytelling is a fundamental activity. It's how we communicate, share experiences, and make sense of the world around us. When applied strategically in the context of social impact, storytelling becomes a potent tool for conveying not only the facts and figures but also the emotions, struggles, and triumphs of those involved in creating positive change.

The power of storytelling lies in its ability to humanize complex issues. It takes data, statistics, and abstract concepts and translates them into relatable narratives that resonate with people on a personal level. When individuals hear stories about the challenges faced by others or the impact of a mission-driven organization's work, they can connect on an emotional level, fostering empathy and understanding.

Stories have a remarkable capacity to inspire action. When people are moved by a compelling narrative, they are more likely to engage, support, or get involved with a cause. Stories create a sense of urgency and purpose, motivating individuals to become part of the solution. Whether it's through volunteering, donating, or advocating for change, storytelling has the power to galvanize individuals into action.

Storytelling is not just about presenting dry facts or statistics, it's about sharing the experiences, struggles, and aspirations of real people. Personal anecdotes and testimonials from those directly affected by a mission's work or those who are actively contributing to a cause bring authenticity and depth to the narrative.

In addition to conveying the impact of social change, storytelling also serves as a bridge that connects organizations with their communities. It enables mission-driven organizations to share their values, missions, and visions in a relatable and memorable way. Through stories, organizations can build trust and loyalty among their stakeholders, fostering a sense of community, connection, and shared purpose.

For mission-driven organizations, crafting compelling stories is an essential part of their communication strategy. It involves identifying the most compelling aspects of their work, profiling the individuals they serve or collaborate with, and conveying the broader societal impact of their mission. It's about using narrative techniques to engage, inform, and mobilize their audience.

## The Imperative Role of Empowerment

Empowerment is the core driving force behind the influence of the social element. It is the transformative energy that propels us to not only engage with other people but also to take meaningful actions that can reshape the world. This empowerment is deeply intertwined with the sense of belonging and connection that people derive from their social interactions.

When individuals feel a genuine sense of belonging within a community, they experience a powerful shift in their mindset. They move from being passive observers to active participants. This transformation is driven by the understanding that their thoughts, actions, and contributions matter and are valued within the group. This newfound sense of purpose and significance empowers them to step forward as leaders, advocates, and changemakers.

The empowerment derived from strong social connections extends far beyond our digital spaces. Empowered individuals take their passion and sense of purpose into the real world, where they can make a tangible impact. They become champions of causes, rallying support, and driving change in their communities and beyond.

This real-world impact can manifest in various ways. Empowered individuals may initiate grassroots movements, organize community events, or lend their voices to advocacy campaigns. They recognize the power of collective action and understand that their social connections provide a support network that amplifies their efforts.

The empowerment stemming from the social element is not limited to a select few. It is a force that can spread like wildfire, inspiring others to take action as well. When one person within a community takes a bold step, it serves as a beacon of possibility for others, encouraging them to do the same. This can lead to a cascade of positive change that reverberates throughout a local, regional, or global community.

In essence, the social element's true power lies in its ability to empower individuals to be agents of change. It is the nucleus that ignites passion, encourages action, and amplifies voices. This empowerment knows no boundaries, as it seamlessly transcends our digital worlds and radiates into the physical world, where it fuels inspiration that bring about tangible transformations. It is a force that reminds us of the incredible impact that strong social connections can have on our lives and the world around us.

# Element 2: Partnerships

The second element of the SPH model is the **partnerships element**. This includes how you partner up, whom you partner up with, and how you keep up these crucial relationships. Again, this may seem obvious, but the types of partnerships and how those partnerships look are changing, along with the expectations of these partnerships. Leveraging community, amplifying storytelling, and measuring joint impact are valuable pieces of the partnership element that we will be exploring.

### The Changing Landscape of Partnerships

Partnerships, throughout history, have been fundamental drivers of progress and growth, fostering collaboration and synergy among individuals, organizations, and even nations. These alliances have historically been characterized by shared interests, mutual goals, and face-to-face interactions. However, the advent of digital and social media has revolutionized the very essence of partnerships, ushering in a new era of connectivity and reshaping the dynamics of collaboration.

We have witnessed a seismic shift in how partnerships are conceived, formed, and maintained. Technology, in particular, has played a pivotal role in this transformation. The emergence of the internet, social media platforms, and advanced communication tools has facilitated connections across vast geographical distances.

No longer bound by physical proximity, individuals and organizations can now effortlessly initiate partnerships with counterparts from diverse corners of the globe.

This democratization of partnerships has leveled the playing field, enabling start-ups, small enterprises, and individuals to engage with global entities on more equal terms. In the past, partnerships often demanded extensive resources, including travel and face-to-face meetings. Now, collaboration is possible with a simple click of a button. The barriers to entry have evaporated, allowing for a broader and more diverse range of partners.

Globalization, another hallmark of our digitally connected world, has further fueled the evolution of partnerships. Businesses, nonprofits, and individuals increasingly engage in collaborations that transcend borders. These global partnerships offer access to diverse markets, resources, and expertise. However, they also introduce new complexities, such as navigating different regulations, cultures, and expectations.

## The Digital Revolution

The digitization of the world has unleashed a transformation in the way partnerships are formed and sustained, primarily through the widespread use of the internet, social media, and advanced communication technologies. These tools have affected the landscape of collaboration, introducing new opportunities and challenges that have redefined the dynamics of partnerships.

Today, technology has acted as a great equalizer, leveling the playing field for partnerships. This democratization of partnerships has had real implications for traditional power dynamics. In the past, established organizations with vast resources often held the upper hand in negotiations and collaborations. However, the influence of traditional power structures has waned as smaller players gain access to global networks and markets. This shift has given rise to more diverse and equitable partnerships, where innovative ideas and unique perspectives are valued alongside financial might.

Although the democratization of partnerships is undoubtedly empowering, it also presents new challenges. The sheer volume of potential collaborators can be overwhelming, making it crucial to navigate these connections with discernment and strategic intent. Additionally, the lack of physical presence and face-to-face interactions can sometimes pose challenges in building trust and rapport.

## Shifting Expectations

A significant shift in expectations has emerged as a defining characteristic of our digital transformation. Gone are the days when partnerships were primarily transactional arrangements, driven solely by financial considerations. In this new era, partnerships are expected to be more than just profit-oriented collaborations; they are increasingly viewed as vehicles for positive change and social responsibility.

This transformation in partnership expectations is driven by a changing societal mindset. Consumers, investors, and employees are no longer content with passive participation in the economy; they seek alignment with organizations and partnerships that reflect their values and beliefs. They demand more than just products or services; they demand purpose and a commitment to broader social and environmental goals.

The concept of *shared value* partnerships embodies this evolution. In shared value partnerships, the emphasis extends beyond mere profit generation. Instead, these collaborations seek to create a positive societal impact alongside economic benefits. This dual focus enables partners to address pressing global challenges while also achieving their business objectives.

Shared value partnerships often are based on themes like sustainability, ethics, and social responsibility. These partnerships leverage the combined resources, expertise, and reach of collaborating entities to effect positive change. For instance, a corporation may partner with a nonprofit organization to address environmental issues, combining their strengths to drive sustainability initiatives and reduce their ecological footprint.

Transparency and accountability are critical pillars of shared value partnerships. Partners are expected to be transparent about their goals, actions, and impacts. This transparency not only builds trust among stakeholders but also holds partners accountable for their commitments. It ensures that the partnership is genuinely delivering on its promises and making a tangible difference.

In this context, purpose-driven actions become paramount. Partnerships are expected to go beyond mere token gestures and deliver meaningful outcomes that align with their stated purpose. This may involve initiatives like responsible sourcing, community engagement, or contributions to social causes.

## Element 3: Human

The third element of the SPH model is the **human element**. Social impact is, by default, the impact that either an organization or a person has on *something*. That something may be a group of people or the planet. Connecting humanity in social impact, sharing the stories of the people behind and in front of the mission, and creating opportunities to build community on the human element will help advance impact and storytelling for any mission-driven organization.

## The Heart of Social Impact

In impact work, there exists a central truth: it is the actions of individuals and organizations that propel positive change. At the heart of these initiatives lies the recognition that social impact extends its reach, nurturing not only the well-being of people but also the health of the planet. The human element embarks on a journey to explore the pivotal role that individuals and organizations play in the creation of social impact, emphasizing the dual focus on people and the planet as the core of mission-driven efforts.

At its essence, social impact is a reflection of the choices, actions, and contributions of those who dedicate themselves to driving change. It is the outcome of the collective aspirations and efforts of individuals who strive to address pressing societal and environmental challenges. Whether driven by a desire to alleviate poverty, combat climate change, promote equality, or support countless other causes, it is people who form the lifeblood of social impact.

Individuals who commit their time, expertise, and resources to effecting positive change are the driving force behind mission-driven organizations. These individuals, often guided by a deep sense of purpose and a commitment to a mission's values, become the architects of initiatives that aim to transform lives and protect the planet. Their dedication fuels innovation, inspires action, and embodies the principle that every positive change begins with a single step.

The heart of social impact is the recognition that the challenges we face today are multilayered. It is the acknowledgment that our actions as individuals and organizations can bring about positive change that not only uplifts communities but also protects and rejuvenates the earth's ecosystems.

## Humanizing Impact

Statistics and data can paint a compelling picture of progress and change. Yet, it is the power of personal narratives that breathes life into these numbers, making the impact tangible, relatable, and deeply meaningful. The human element delves into the transformative influence of personal stories in conveying the genuine impact of missions and underscores the importance of sharing narratives from those behind and in front of the mission—illuminating the experiences, motivations, and human elements that drive these initiatives.

Personal stories possess a unique ability to touch the hearts and minds of audiences in a way that statistics and reports cannot. Although data can provide valuable insights into the scale and scope of social impact, it is personal narratives that imbue these figures with emotion, context, and resonance. Stories have an inherent capacity to bridge the gap between abstract concepts and lived experiences, enabling people to connect on a deeper level.

Take my cancer journey and Make-A-Wish story. These experiences help to make abstract concepts tangible, reminding us that behind every statistic or mission, there are real people with unique stories and emotions. These stories connect a mission's objectives and the hearts and minds of your current and prospective supporters.

One of the remarkable aspects of personal stories is their universality. They transcend geographical boundaries, cultural differences, and socioeconomic disparities. A story from a small village in a remote part of the world can resonate just as deeply with someone on the opposite side of the globe. This universality of storytelling makes it a powerful tool for building empathy, fostering understanding, and uniting people in the pursuit of common goals.

Personal narratives bring the human element into sharp focus. These narratives humanize the larger mission, showcasing the real people who are affected by it and those who dedicate themselves to its realization.

When we delve into the experiences of individuals directly affected by a mission, we gain insights into the transformative effects of these initiatives on their lives. Personal stories reveal the challenges overcome, the aspirations achieved, and the resilience displayed by those who have benefited. They provide a face and a voice to the statistics, enabling us to see the real people whose lives have been changed for the better.

Conversely, when we explore the stories of individuals behind the mission—the visionaries, the activists, the changemakers—we gain an understanding of the motivations and passions that drive them. These stories showcase the dedication, sacrifice, and unwavering commitment of those who have made it their life's work to effect positive change. They serve as a source of inspiration for others, demonstrating that individuals have the power to create meaningful impact.

## Using Empathy to Enact Change

Empathy stands as a potent force capable of driving meaningful and lasting change. It is the ability to understand and share the feelings, experiences, and perspectives of others that empowers individuals and organizations to connect deeply with a mission. The human element discusses the pivotal role of empathy in the context of social impact and how understanding the human element of a mission can inspire action and mobilize support.

Empathy, often described as the capacity to walk in someone else's shoes, is a fundamental trait of human nature. It enables individuals to connect with the experiences and emotions of others, fostering a sense of shared humanity.

One of the key functions of empathy is to break down the barriers that often separate individuals from the missions they wish to support. It enables people to see beyond statistics and data, connecting them to the real people whose lives are touched by these missions. When individuals understand the challenges, aspirations, and emotions of those affected, they are more likely to feel a personal connection and a sense of responsibility to act.

Empathy serves as a bridge between awareness and action. When individuals genuinely empathize with the struggles and triumphs of others, they are motivated to take meaningful steps to effect change. This might involve volunteering time and resources, advocating for policy changes, or simply raising awareness about a particular cause. Empathy transforms passive observers into active participants in the journey toward social impact.

Empathy can also have a magnetic effect, inspiring others to join in the mission. When individuals witness the compassionate actions of their peers, they are more likely to be motivated to contribute as well. This chain reaction can lead to a groundswell of support, amplifying the mission's reach and impact.

Understanding the human element of a mission is central to inspiring empathy. It involves sharing personal stories, experiences, and perspectives to create a vivid and relatable narrative. These stories provide the context and emotional connection necessary for individuals to grasp the significance of the mission and the impact it has on real people.

These narratives humanize the statistics, allowing donors and supporters to empathize with the challenges faced by these families. As a result, individuals are more likely to contribute resources, volunteer their time, or advocate for policies that address the missions they support.

# Navigating the Future

As you navigate this book, keep in mind that this three-element philosophy has been forged with the goal of answering the question, "How can we navigate the future of social impact?," and, importantly, what we need to pay attention to, to prepare for the rapidly changing landscape. Take notes, make connections, and hopefully you find these concepts relatable and applicable to your impact work and perspective.

On that note, let's dive in!

# Social

Harnessing the power of social, partnership, and human elements is crucial to driving positive change and building thriving communities for good. The SPH model serves as a blueprint for achieving these objectives and maximizing social impact.

In this comprehensive exploration, we embark on a journey through the first element of the SPH model: the social component. This foundational aspect is all about creating social moments, forging connections, and empowering communities for the greater good. It encompasses the art of communication, the ability to connect with people on a deeper level, and the strategic participation in activities that foster unity and engagement.

Being social in this context extends far beyond casual small talk or virtual likes and shares. It signifies a purpose-driven approach to connecting with others, one that promotes positive communication, meaningful interactions, and active engagement. These are the building blocks of community formation, a fundamental element of driving social impact.

To understand the significance of being social, it's essential to delve into the core principles that underpin effective community building. It involves fostering an environment of inclusivity, where individuals from diverse backgrounds and perspectives feel welcome and valued. It's about cultivating a culture of empathy and active listening, where people genuinely connect and understand each other's experiences and aspirations.

The influence of social media on our lives is undeniable. It has revolutionized the way we connect, communicate, and engage with the world. It has also emerged as a powerful tool for social impact, offering individuals, businesses, and nonprofits unparalleled opportunities to amplify their voices and mobilize communities for change.

Part I's discussion of this element of the SPH model delves into the pivotal role of social media in the pursuit of social impact. It recognizes that social media is already deeply ingrained in our lives, and its significance will only continue to grow as algorithms evolve and platforms expand. Therefore, understanding how to harness its potential is paramount for anyone seeking to increase their social impact.

Leveraging social media for social impact involves a comprehensive approach that encompasses storytelling, community building, and influencer collaboration.

At the heart of social media's impact lies the art of storytelling. Storytelling has the unique ability to convey the human element of social impact. It transforms facts and data into relatable narratives that resonate with people on an emotional level. Throughout Part I, we explore how to craft compelling stories that connect individuals to missions and causes, inspiring action and fostering empathy.

Building and nurturing online communities is also a central pillar of social media's potential for social impact. These communities provide a space for like-minded individuals to connect, share experiences, and collaborate on initiatives that drive positive change. We delve into strategies for creating and growing these communities, fostering a sense of belonging and shared purpose among members.

Collaborating with influencers is a powerful strategy for expanding the reach and impact of social initiatives. Influencers possess the ability to sway opinions, spark conversations, and mobilize their followers toward social causes. We explore the art of influencer partnerships, from identifying the right influencers to aligning their values and missions.

The social aspect of the SPH model lays the foundation for a holistic approach to social impact. It recognizes that meaningful change cannot occur in isolation; it requires the interconnectedness of individuals, organizations, and communities.

By understanding the nuances of being social in a purpose-driven sense, leveraging the influence of social media, and mastering the art of storytelling, community building, and influencer collaboration, individuals and organizations can unlock the transformative potential of the social element of the SPH model.

# 1

# Storytelling and Socializing

Social media has evolved into an unparalleled environment for interactions, connecting individuals and organizations across the globe. With more than 4.5 billion social media users worldwide, these platforms have become a gold mine for those seeking to broaden their social circles, amplify their impact, and discover new philanthropic opportunities. For mission-driven organizations, harnessing the power of social media is not merely an option, it is an imperative. At the heart of this digital revolution lies the art of storytelling—a potent tool for building connections, fostering engagement, and driving social change.

The ubiquity of social media in today's world cannot be overstated. It has fundamentally transformed how we communicate, share information, and engage with each other. Whether through Facebook, Twitter, Instagram, LinkedIn, TikTok, or emerging platforms like Twitch, social media provides a virtual meeting ground where people from diverse backgrounds and locations converge to connect, converse, and collaborate.

For mission-driven organizations, social media presents a vast landscape of opportunities. It serves as a dynamic platform to convey their stories, missions, and values to a global audience. These platforms also enable organizations to engage with their supporters, foster a sense of community, and mobilize individuals toward shared objectives.

At the heart of social media's potential for mission-driven organizations lies the art of storytelling. Effective storytelling transforms mission statements, data, and facts into compelling narratives that resonate with audiences on a personal level. It humanizes complex issues, connects individuals to a cause, and inspires action.

The process of honing the power of storytelling begins with crafting a compelling narrative—a story that encapsulates the organization's mission, values, and impact. This narrative should be clear, concise, and emotionally resonant, inviting individuals to become part of the journey. It should be a story that engages, evokes empathy, and elicits a desire to contribute to positive change.

Storytelling versatility is also key. Each platform offers a unique ecosystem with its own audience, culture, and communication style. Mission-driven organizations must not only hone their story but also adapt it for each platform.

Refreshing the narrative regularly is essential to maintain relevance and captivate an ever-evolving social media audience. Timely updates ensure that the story remains compelling and aligned with current events and trends. It demonstrates an organization's adaptability and commitment to staying engaged with its supporters.

Adapting the story for each platform recognizes the distinct preferences and behaviors of users on various social media platforms. For instance, a visually engaging story may resonate well on Instagram, whereas a more professionally oriented narrative may find its audience on LinkedIn. Understanding these nuances enables organizations to tailor their storytelling to maximize impact. By honing their stories, refreshing them regularly, and adapting them for each platform, mission-driven organizations can harness the full potential of social media, effectively connecting with their audience and driving meaningful change in the world.

## Impactful Storytelling

Social media has emerged as an incredibly potent tool for driving social impact, offering unparalleled opportunities for rapid information dissemination, community building, and the amplification of meaningful messages. Compared to pre–social media, when a message would have to be printed and published all over the city to be seen, requiring time-consuming and resource-intensive efforts, social media enables a message to reach a targeted audience within seconds. This transformative capability has redefined how individuals and organizations approach advocacy and impact-driven initiatives.

The evolution of advocacy and social impact through social media is nothing short of remarkable. It has ushered in a time where a single tweet, post, or video can spark global conversations, raise awareness about critical issues, mobilize communities, or even build momentum for revolutions. This newfound speed and reach are a testament to the democratization of information and the power of digital connectivity. Social media has shattered barriers, enabling anyone with an internet connection to become a messenger for their cause.

One of the defining features of social media's impact on advocacy is its capacity for rapid information dissemination.

A message, whether it's a call for social justice, an environmental alert, or a humanitarian plea, can be shared globally with a click of a button. This speed is invaluable in addressing urgent issues, such as disaster relief, when immediate action is crucial.

Consider the example of disaster response. Social media platforms enable organizations to swiftly share information about emergencies, coordinate relief efforts, and connect with volunteers and donors. The real-time nature of these platforms empowers individuals and organizations to respond to crises more efficiently and effectively than ever before.

Through these small interactions and conversations, there lies exponential opportunities to cultivate and develop impact. A small thread can generate unprecedented momentum, all rooted in the power of impactful storytelling.

Let's examine the #MeToo movement. It began with a simple hashtag on social media, where individuals shared their personal stories of sexual harassment and assault. These stories resonated with millions, sparking a global conversation about gender-based violence and discrimination. The movement's success hinged on the power of storytelling to connect individuals with a shared experience and a common goal.

Impactful storytelling on social media requires careful consideration of several key elements: authenticity, emotion, visual appeal, engagement, and consistency.

## Authenticity

Authenticity stands as an essential characteristic of storytelling. It's the genuine, unfiltered, and unapologetic sharing of stories and experiences that resonates most with audiences. In a social media landscape inundated with curated content and carefully crafted personas, authenticity shines as a beacon of trust and credibility.

Audiences on social media are discerning and astute. They can swiftly distinguish between authentic narratives and content driven by ulterior motives. It's the raw and unvarnished stories that capture hearts and minds, forging deep connections between storytellers and their audiences.

When individuals and organizations authentically share their experiences, challenges, and triumphs, they invite others into their world. This transparency fosters trust, as audiences perceive a genuine commitment to openness and honesty. Authenticity humanizes the storyteller, making them relatable and approachable, while also reflecting a level of vulnerability that resonates with people's own experiences.

## Emotion

Emotion is the heartbeat of impactful storytelling. It has the ability to bridge the gap between a narrative and its audience, transforming a story into a compelling call to action. Whether it's the stirring sensation of empathy, the warm embrace of hope, or the fiery spark of indignation, emotion forms the connective tissue that binds individuals to a cause and fuels their motivation to effect change.

Empathy is a powerful motivator for action. A story that triggers empathy invites the audience to step into the shoes of those directly affected by an issue, prompting a visceral understanding of their struggles and aspirations. This emotional resonance often drives individuals to extend a helping hand or advocate for justice on behalf of those in need.

Hope, however, offers a beacon of optimism amidst challenges. Stories imbued with hope inspire individuals by showcasing the potential for positive change and the possibility of a brighter future. These narratives empower people to contribute to a cause, believing that their actions can make a meaningful difference.

Indignation, driven by stories that expose injustice or wrongdoing, stirs individuals to take a stand. It fuels a sense of moral obligation and compels action in the face of societal ills. When people are emotionally moved by tales of injustice, they are driven to advocate for reform, raise their voices, and push for systemic change.

## Visual Appeal

Visual content, encompassing images and videos, possesses a unique ability to captivate and resonate with audiences, elevating the impact of storytelling to new heights. The human brain is naturally predisposed to rapidly and efficiently process visual information. When paired with a compelling narrative, visuals create a holistic storytelling experience that not only captures attention but also enhances understanding and retention. Visuals provide context, evoke emotions, and simplify complex concepts, making them accessible to a broader audience.

Visuals also have a shareability factor that is unparalleled. When users encounter scroll-stopping images or engaging videos on social media, they are more inclined to share this content with their own networks. Sharing amplifies the reach of the story, enabling it to circulate through social media platforms and reach a wider audience than text alone could achieve.

Consider the impact of a heartwarming image that illustrates the positive outcome of a charity or a video showcasing the transformative journey of an individual or community. These visuals not only grab viewers' attention but also elicit emotions: joy, empathy, or inspiration. Consequently, these visuals motivate viewers to engage with the content, share it with their connections, and participate in the mission or cause being highlighted.

## Engagement

Interactivity is an indispensable ingredient in the recipe for effective social media storytelling. It transcends passive consumption, transforming narratives into dynamic and engaging experiences. Encouraging audience participation through comments, shares, and discussions is like inviting them into the storytelling process, building a sense of ownership while enabling a multitude of benefits that extend the reach and impact of the narrative.

When audiences are encouraged to actively engage with a narrative through comments, they become cocreators of the story. Their input adds layers of perspective, insight, and personal connection that enhance the richness of the narrative. Discussions that ensue not only amplify the message but also foster a sense of community around the story, connecting like-minded individuals and sparking dialogue.

Shares are the digital equivalent of word-of-mouth recommendations. When individuals resonate with a narrative and share it within their own networks, the story's reach expands exponentially, reaching audiences far beyond the original storyteller's sphere of influence. Each share is a personal endorsement, a vote of confidence in the narrative's importance, and a testament to its impact.

Interactivity also nurtures a sense of ownership among the audience members. When people feel their opinions and voices are valued, they are more likely to become advocates for the cause or mission. They feel invested in the narrative's success and motivated to take meaningful actions to support it.

## Consistency

Consistency in storytelling is the compass that guides a narrative through our rapidly changing social landscape. In social media, where trends come and go in minutes, maintaining a regular presence is vital to ensuring a message's ongoing relevance and impact. This consistency is achieved through regular updates and the infusion of fresh, engaging content.

A narrative that remains static risks fading into the background. To capture and sustain audience attention, it's crucial to provide a continuous stream of content that not only aligns with the core message but also adapts to the shifting dynamics of the platform and the interests of the audience.

Regular updates serve as checkpoints along the storytelling journey. They keep the narrative alive and responsive to current events, emerging trends, and evolving audience preferences. They also reinforce the organization's commitment to the cause or mission, showcasing its enduring dedication.

Fresh content injects vitality into the narrative, preventing it from becoming stale or repetitive. It introduces new perspectives, angles, and stories that resonate with existing followers and potential newcomers. These additions breathe life into the message, keeping it vibrant and engaging.

Consistency in storytelling is not about monotonous repetition but about strategic evolution. It's about maintaining the essence of the narrative while allowing it to grow and adapt. Through this dynamic approach, a message remains not only compelling but also relevant over time, ensuring its enduring impact.

## The Medium Is the Message

"It's not what you say, it's how you say it." This timeless adage holds immense relevance in today's social media landscape, where storytelling is a dynamic force that varies in impact depending on where and how it's delivered. Social media platforms are like diverse stages, each with its own audience, expectations, and consumption patterns. Understanding this fundamental truth and applying it strategically is imperative for mission-driven organizations seeking to create awareness, build advocates and community, and ultimately expand their impact.

Consider this scenario: a short video on TikTok garners 1 million views and sparks a flurry of engagement, while the same video posted on Instagram struggles to gain traction, receiving minimal attention. Why does this discrepancy exist? It's because our expectations and consumption patterns differ depending on the platform. Each social media stage has its own unique audience, culture, and communication style.

For mission-driven organizations, this variability in audience behavior is a crucial consideration. When crafting and delivering their stories, they must be mindful of where and how they share them. The same story may need to be adapted and presented differently on Facebook, Instagram, TikTok, LinkedIn, or Twitter to resonate with the respective audiences. For example, an organization that wants to raise money to build a new animal shelter might highlight prominent donors on LinkedIn, upload funny videos to TikTok of rescued animals doing amazing things, post weekly profiles of new animals for adoption on Facebook, and tweet about the ongoing status of fundraising for the shelter.

In storytelling, stagnation is the enemy of impact. When was the last time your organization refreshed its story? Have you explored different ways of telling it? Your mission story underpins your outreach, engagement, and growth. It serves as the foundation on which you build awareness, cultivate advocates, and foster a sense of community.

The best place to start when refreshing your story is to begin by revisiting the why. Why should people outside of your organization care? The why should be bold, audacious, and inspiring—a challenge that instills both fear and joy, where the challenge itself is daunting, but the impact and results of your work are rewarding. Starting with an abundance mindset and breaking your story into digestible bite-sized pieces is a strategic approach. These concise narratives serve as building blocks, offering flexibility in tailoring your message to different platforms and audiences.

Each social media platform has its unique characteristics, catering to distinct audience preferences. To effectively convey your refreshed story, align these small, more snackable versions with the most suitable platforms.

For instance, if your current audience predominantly engages on Facebook, consider that this platform's audience tends to engage with longer-form videos and posts. Craft your narrative accordingly, emphasizing depth and detail. Alternatively, if you're focused on growing your Instagram audience, leverage poignant and direct elements of your story to accompany emotionally resonant images or short videos, capitalizing on the platform's visual nature.

Local events and partnerships offer yet another avenue for tailoring your story. Suppose your organization collaborates with a local business for a happy hour event. In that case, you can extract localized components of your story to make it relatable to the event's attendees, enhancing engagement and forging deeper connections.

Ultimately, the venue—whether virtual or physical—matters to storytelling. By recalibrating, reconstructing, and reviewing your narrative through the lens of location, audience, and perspective, you unlock the potential to build new relationships, strengthen existing ones, and unearth novel ways of sustaining community engagement.

## Creating Social Moments

It's important to reiterate that not all places and platforms are the same when it comes to engagement through storytelling, nor do you need to be everyone all the time. In order to create truly memorable, long-lasting social moments, it's important to take account of where you are at in your organization's life cycle, what the major needs of the organization are, and what your organization's goals are. Too often an organization takes a wide-aim approach because of the perceived need to be on multiple platforms all the time. And because we are all so focused on being everywhere digitally, we completely forget the importance of socializing in real life (IRL). This is why we suggest that, to be present in your social initiatives, follow this simple formula for truly impactful social moments: Mission + Message + Medium = Inspiration

Defining your target audience starts with answering these questions:

- Where are you at in your organization's life cycle?
- What are your organization's major needs?
- What are your organization's goals?
- Are you just launching or are you focused on expansion or growth?

Understanding, and being realistic about, the stage your organization is at is important in determining your target audience. If you are just starting out, then maybe your target audience is your initial advisors/board members and their network. If you are looking to expand, then maybe your target audience is an underrepresented segment of supporters.

Needs of an organization go far beyond financial. Activating social moments and refining your target audience is all about understanding the organization's needs. Some great thought starters for needs identification are questions such as these:

- Are people aware of who we are and what we do?
- Do we need more people interested in who we are and what we do?
- Are we converting enough interested people to take action?

Awareness is usually the first and most pressing need and persists regardless of the life cycle of an organization.

As you home in on the organization's needs, you can also begin to create goals that align with those needs. Creating more awareness might translate to increasing social media followers or visitors to your website. Generating more interest might be finding ways to add more people to your mailing list. For converting interest to action, it might be improving your average donation amount per newsletter contact. These represent just a small sampling of potential goals, but ensure that the goals align with the needs of your organization.

Once you've determined your target audience, and how you can apply your story to your target audience, it is time to create social moments. Focus on the venue where the majority of your target audience engages and interacts, and where you can create the most joint value for them and your mission. The first inclination is to move to social media, which may be best, but do not underestimate the value of in-person social moments. Creating in person moments usually creates amazing storytelling content that can be repurposed and reshared on social platforms. Social moments aren't about size but about reaching your target for a desired impact.

For example, if you are just starting your organization, social movements can help to build deeper relationships with existing supporters (remember: nurturing relationships is just as important as creating new ones). Social moments can be used to mobilize supporters and encourage them to take action, such as by signing petitions, volunteering, or even bringing in new supporters. Before social media, this was much more challenging to do because communication was limited to what could be done within a limited network. Now social media can be used as your megaphone for these social moments. The social media platform that you opt for will differ depending on the goals you have. For example, Instagram is an optional platform for visual content, or if your organization is providing hourly information, Twitter might be best.

Different social media platforms offer a variety of features and capabilities. Currently, the most popular social media platforms include Facebook, Instagram, X (formerly known as Twitter), LinkedIn, TikTok, and YouTube, but dedicated streaming platforms like Twitch are also important when considering social media platforms.

## Facebook

Facebook, a long-standing and iconic social media platform, continues to play a prominent role in the social media landscape. Its enduring popularity stems from its ability to cater to a wide range of user demographics and preferences.

One distinguishing feature of Facebook is its appeal to an older demographic. Although younger generations have flocked to newer platforms, Facebook remains a preferred choice for a more mature audience. This demographic diversity is a strategic advantage for mission-driven organizations seeking to engage with a broad spectrum of supporters. Whether your cause resonates with Millennials, Generation X, or Baby Boomers, Facebook provides a versatile platform to reach and connect with your target demographic.

One of Facebook's standout features is its robust community-building tool: Facebook Groups. These digital gathering places serve as hubs for like-minded individuals who come together to discuss shared interests, causes, hobbies, or even educational pursuits. For mission-driven organizations, Facebook Groups offer a powerful tool to foster engagement, dialogue, and collaboration among supporters.

Online course leaders, in particular, have found Facebook Groups to be invaluable in their efforts to facilitate meaningful interactions among participants. These groups serve as virtual classrooms, where learners can connect with their peers, discuss course content, and receive guidance from instructors. The sense of community that Facebook Groups cultivates can significantly enhance the learning experience and encourage active participation.

Facebook Groups are also versatile and adaptable. They provide a structured environment for organizing events, workshops, and discussions related to your mission. Whether you're rallying supporters for a fundraising campaign, hosting a virtual seminar, or coordinating volunteer efforts, Facebook Groups offer a centralized space for planning, communication, and collaboration.

Another noteworthy aspect of Facebook's enduring popularity is its extensive reach. With billions of active users worldwide, the platform provides a vast audience for mission-driven organizations to tap into. Although it's true that organic reach on Facebook has become more challenging due to algorithmic changes, the platform's advertising capabilities remain an important tool for reaching specific demographics and expanding your organization's visibility.

## Instagram

Instagram, a visual-centric platform, has solidified its position as a social media powerhouse. Boasting over a billion active users worldwide, it has become not only one of the largest but also one of the most profitable platforms for individuals, businesses, and mission-driven organizations to use. Instagram's unique blend of visual storytelling and community building has made it an indispensable tool for reaching, engaging, and mobilizing diverse audiences. For mission-driven organizations, this visual format offers a powerful means of conveying their impact and connecting with their audience.

Instagram's user base skews notably younger, making it a prime platform for engaging with Millennials and Generation Z. These generations often possess a strong sense of social responsibility and are more inclined to support causes and missions that resonate with their values. If your target audience includes young people, Instagram is an ideal space for cultivating meaningful connections and rallying support.

## Twitter (Now Called X)

Twitter (now technically called X), a platform defined by its succinct and rapid-fire nature, has long been a hub for sharing short messages, known as tweets. With its emphasis on brevity and real-time updates, X has become a dynamic space for individuals, organizations, and even world leaders to disseminate news, engage with audiences, and spark discussions. However, it's important to note that the landscape of X continues to rapidly evolve at the time of this writing, given the many changes new owner Elon Musk has been making, which has introduced an element of uncertainty and volatility.

One of X's defining features is its limited character count, with tweets traditionally restricted to 280 characters—unless you are a paying member of their Blue membership. This constraint encourages concise and impactful communication, making it an ideal platform for sharing quick updates, thoughts, and snippets of information. For mission-driven organizations, this can be a valuable tool for delivering key messages and keeping supporters informed about recent developments related to their cause.

The real-time nature of X is another distinctive aspect. Users engage with a live feed of tweets, offering immediate access to breaking news, trending topics, and discussions. This real-time dimension enables organizations to participate in timely conversations, respond to emerging issues, and stay at the forefront of relevant dialogues within their field.

However, given the many uncertainties of the platform, organizations may need to exercise caution when determining their approach to X in the current context. It may be best to closely monitor developments related to the platform's direction before making significant investments in X as a communication channel.

## LinkedIn

LinkedIn, often overlooked when it comes to social media platforms for mission-driven organizations, is a hidden gem that offers unique advantages for building communities and fostering partnerships. This professional networking platform boasts a distinct demographic composition that aligns perfectly with the goals of corporate partnerships, social responsibility initiatives, and mission-driven collaborations.

With its nearly 1 billion users globally, LinkedIn primarily caters to professionals, business leaders, and decision-makers. This demographic composition sets it apart from other social media platforms, making it a hub for individuals who are actively engaged in their careers, committed to corporate social responsibility (CSR), and passionate about supporting meaningful causes.

One of LinkedIn's standout features is its capacity for facilitating connections within the corporate world. This makes it an ideal platform for mission-driven organizations looking to establish and nurture corporate partnerships. Decision-makers and CSR professionals frequently use LinkedIn to network, share insights, and seek out opportunities for collaboration.

Building a community of corporate partners is not only feasible on LinkedIn but also highly advantageous. Mission-driven organizations can leverage the platform to connect with like-minded businesses, engage with corporate leaders, and explore avenues for mutually beneficial collaborations. LinkedIn Groups, in particular, provide a space for fostering meaningful discussions and interactions among professionals interested in CSR and mission-driven initiatives.

Social responsibility is a core focus area on LinkedIn, with many organizations and professionals actively championing various causes. This presents an opportunity for mission-driven organizations to tap into a preexisting community of individuals who are passionate about creating positive social impact.

LinkedIn also provides robust tools for content sharing and thought leadership. Organizations can use the platform to showcase their mission, share success stories, and highlight their impact on the community and society at large. By consistently producing and sharing relevant content, mission-driven organizations can establish themselves as thought leaders in their respective fields, attracting support and engagement from a highly targeted audience.

LinkedIn's professional nature extends to its company pages, where organizations can create a dedicated space to communicate their mission and values. This serves as a central hub for sharing updates, job opportunities, and insights related to the organization's cause. Additionally, LinkedIn's events feature provides a platform for hosting webinars, conferences, and virtual gatherings, enhancing the organization's capacity to engage with its community.

## TikTok

TikTok, the rapidly growing short-form video-sharing platform, has taken the social media world by storm in recent years. This platform allows users to create and share videos that are typically 15 seconds or shorter, making it a unique and engaging space for creative expression and storytelling. Although TikTok has garnered immense popularity, particularly among younger users, it has also become a source of both excitement and controversy.

One of TikTok's defining features is its emphasis on brevity. There is no question that our attention spans are shrinking, and TikTok's bite-sized video format aligns perfectly with the preferences of modern users. This short-form content is not only easy to consume but also encourages creativity, because users must convey their messages and stories within a concise time frame.

TikTok's appeal is driven by its vibrant and diverse community, where users can explore a wide range of content, from humor and entertainment to educational and informative clips. The platform's "For You Page" algorithm uses machine learning to curate a personalized feed for each user, enhancing the chances of content going viral. This algorithmic approach has contributed to TikTok's reputation as a platform where individuals and organizations can quickly gain widespread recognition and engagement.

However, as mentioned, TikTok is not without its share of controversy. Concerns have arisen about the platform's suitability for sourcing credible information. Given its focus on short, often entertaining videos, TikTok may not be the go-to platform for in-depth news and authoritative content. Users should exercise caution and verify information obtained from TikTok before accepting it as fact.

Despite these concerns, TikTok's potential as a platform to have your content go viral should not be underestimated. For mission-driven organizations, TikTok offers an opportunity to reach a broad and engaged audience quickly. Creative storytelling on TikTok can captivate viewers and drive conversations on social causes and initiatives.

Many organizations have successfully harnessed TikTok's trend-driven culture to promote awareness of critical issues. TikTok challenges and trends can serve as a vehicle for spreading messages related to social impact and encouraging users to take action. The platform's collaborative and participatory nature enables organizations to engage with a younger demographic actively interested in making a difference.

Although TikTok may not be the primary platform for sharing in-depth information or comprehensive narratives, it excels in capturing attention and sparking curiosity. Mission-driven organizations can leverage TikTok to pique interest in their causes, directing viewers to more informative resources on other platforms or websites for a deeper understanding of their mission, initiatives, and programs.

## YouTube

YouTube, the long-standing powerhouse of online video content, has established itself as a versatile platform for creators, companies, and mission-driven organizations alike. This digital behemoth boasts an extensive library of videos spanning a wide range of topics, making it a go-to destination for individuals seeking both entertainment and education. For mission-driven organizations, YouTube presents a valuable space for sharing long-form video content, engaging with audiences, and harnessing the power of visual storytelling.

One of YouTube's standout features is its capacity to accommodate a diverse array of content types. Creators on the platform produce videos on everything from tutorials and reviews to vlogs and documentaries. This diversity enables mission-driven organizations to tailor their content to suit their unique messaging and objectives.

YouTube's popularity among content creators and users is further amplified by its status as the second-largest search engine globally, surpassed only by its parent company, Google. This distinction makes YouTube an essential platform for organizations looking to enhance their online visibility and discoverability. By optimizing video titles, descriptions, and tags with relevant keywords, organizations can improve their chances of appearing in search results, effectively driving organic traffic to their content.

For mission-driven organizations, YouTube serves as a dynamic canvas for sharing impactful stories, initiatives, and educational resources. Long-form video content on this platform enables organizations to dive deep into their missions, offering comprehensive insights and perspectives that resonate with their target audiences. This extended format provides ample space for storytelling, enabling organizations to craft compelling narratives that captivate and inspire viewers.

YouTube's user-friendly interface empowers organizations to create and maintain dedicated channels, where all their video content can be organized and easily accessible to viewers. These channels serve as centralized hubs for presenting the organization's mission, showcasing success stories, and fostering a sense of community among subscribers and supporters.

Another advantage of YouTube is its robust analytics and engagement metrics. Organizations can gain valuable insights into how viewers are interacting with, and finding, their content, including metrics such as view count, watch time, audience demographics, and traffic sources. These data-driven insights enable organizations to refine their content strategy, ensuring that their videos effectively resonate with their target audience.

YouTube's comment section fosters two-way communication between organizations and their viewers. This interactive feature enables organizations to receive feedback, answer questions, and engage in meaningful dialogues with their community. Additionally, live streaming on YouTube offers real-time engagement opportunities, enabling organizations to connect with their audience during live events, webinars, and Q&A sessions.

By using YouTube's features, analytics, and interactive tools, mission-driven organizations can not only amplify their impact but also forge deeper connections with their community. As they continue to harness the power of visual storytelling, YouTube remains a compelling space for organizations to make their voices heard and inspire positive social transformation.

## Twitch

Many other social media platforms offer different features and capabilities. One of growing importance from a demographics and content perspective is Twitch. The emergence of Twitch as a powerful social media platform has been marked by record-breaking achievements, particularly during the early days of the pandemic when tens of millions of dollars were raised by Twitch content creators. This platform's continued growth and use represent a significant shift in how individuals and organizations engage with new demographics and explore fresh avenues for storytelling.

Twitch is a live streaming platform primarily focused on video game streaming and esports. It was launched in 2011 and has since gained immense popularity, becoming one of the most prominent platforms for gamers and content creators. What sets Twitch apart from traditional social media platforms is its emphasis on real-time, live content, which fosters genuine interactions between creators and viewers.

One of the key reasons for Twitch's growing importance is its ability to appeal to a diverse range of demographics. Although initially recognized as a hub for gaming enthusiasts, Twitch has expanded its content beyond gaming-related broadcasts. Today, you can find channels dedicated to music, art, cooking, fitness, and even IRL streams that capture various aspects of a creator's daily life.

Twitch's demographic diversity is particularly appealing for mission-driven organizations aiming to reach and engage with new audiences. Unlike some other platforms that may skew toward specific age groups or interests, Twitch offers a broader spectrum of viewers, providing opportunities to connect with individuals who might not be active on other social media sites.

What sets Twitch apart is its live interaction and engagement features. Creators stream in real time, allowing viewers to participate in live chats, ask questions, and interact with the streamer directly. This live engagement fosters a sense of community and connection, making viewers feel like active participants rather than passive observers.

For mission-driven organizations, this live interaction is a powerful tool for building rapport, fostering a sense of belonging, and conveying the urgency and authenticity of their mission. Whether it's hosting live Q&A sessions, showcasing behind-the-scenes operations, or discussing important issues, Twitch provides a dynamic platform for direct engagement.

During the early days of the COVID-19 pandemic, Twitch emerged as a platform for fundraising and philanthropic efforts. Content creators organized charity streams, encouraging their viewers to donate to various causes. The results were astounding, with tens of millions of dollars raised for a wide range of charitable initiatives.

The success of charity streams on Twitch highlights the platform's potential as a fundraising tool for mission-driven organizations. The live nature of the platform allows for real-time donation tracking and acknowledgment, creating a sense of immediate impact for donors. This direct link between content creators and their communities contributes to the generosity and philanthropic spirit witnessed on the platform.

Twitch's interactive and real-time nature also opens up innovative storytelling opportunities. Creators can use the platform to share narratives, showcase the impact of their work, and create immersive experiences for their audience. Here are some examples:

- **Live campaign updates.** Organizations can host live broadcasts to provide real-time updates on their initiatives, showcasing progress, sharing success stories, and addressing challenges.

- **Documentary-style streams.** Creators can produce documentary-style content that delves deep into the mission and activities of a mission-driven organization, offering viewers an in-depth look at their work.

- **Collaborative efforts.** Twitch enables collaborations between content creators and mission-driven organizations. These partnerships can result in unique content, fundraising events, and broader community engagement.

- **Advocacy and awareness.** Organizations can leverage the platform to raise awareness about their cause, educate viewers about important issues, and advocate for change in real time.

Social media has become an essential tool for mission-driven organizations, offering opportunities to connect, engage, and mobilize a global audience. At its core, the power of social media for these organizations lies in the art of storytelling, which has the capacity to transform data into compelling narratives that inspire personal connections and drive meaningful action.

CHAPTER

# 2

# Community and Connection

Storytelling and community building are the dynamic forces that propel mission-driven organizations toward meaningful impact. In the social portion of the SPH model, where connection is the foundational principle, storytelling and community take center stage as essential tools for scaling impact. Three critical areas—awareness, interest, and action—serve as the strategic pillars through which storytelling and community are harnessed to drive change and create lasting, positive effects in the world.

## The Seed of Connection: Storytelling

Storytelling, often referred to as the soul of an organization, serves as the seed from which connections and communities flourish. At its core, storytelling is about forging a common connection point, a thread that binds individuals with shared values, aspirations, and concerns. It's the means through which mission-driven organizations communicate their purpose, impact, and vision to the world.

However, storytelling is not just a tool for transmitting information; it's a vehicle for creating a sense of connection. It engages the heart and the mind, evoking emotions and empathy that bridge the gap between an organization and its audience. It humanizes the mission, transforming abstract goals into relatable narratives that people can connect with.

Yet, awareness, the initial stage of connection building, is often overlooked or underappreciated in the pursuit of tangible outcomes. Many organizations tend to prioritize financial objectives and direct action while undervaluing the foundational role of awareness. This oversight can limit the depth and breadth of community engagement and hinder long-term impact.

To fully harness the power of storytelling and community, organizations must recognize the pivotal role of awareness. Greater awareness serves as the entry point to engagement and action. It's the first step in the journey of connecting with individuals who share an affinity for a cause.

Building awareness is sowing the seeds of connection. Begin modestly and consistently, nurturing the growth of awareness like a budding plant. Storytelling can be amplified through various channels, from social media platforms to email newsletters and blogs. Each piece of content, each narrative shared, contributes to the expansion of awareness.

Visibility and awareness are not static; they are additive. As awareness grows, it generates momentum. Harness social moments and sustained storytelling to deepen connections and pique interest among your audience. Storytelling should be a continuous process, adapting to changing circumstances and the evolving needs of the community.

Growing awareness sets the stage for fostering a sense of community and, in turn, generating interest in supporting an organization's mission. When individuals become aware of a cause and feel a connection, their interest in that mission is piqued. This interest signifies a willingness to engage, contribute, and participate actively.

Effective storytelling plays a pivotal role in creating these deeper connections. It invites individuals to step closer to the cause, delve into its nuances, and understand its impact. Storytelling humanizes the mission, making it relatable and emotionally resonant.

Action, at its essence, is the manifestation of interest. When people feel genuinely connected to a cause, they are more inclined to get involved and support it. The greater the connection, the stronger the interest, and this interest activates the three critical Ts of impact: time, talent, and treasure.

## The Three Ts of Impact: Time, Talent, and Treasure

At its core, impact is defined by action. However, there are no shortcuts to inspiring action. To unlock the full potential of supporters' contributions, it is essential to dedicate attention to consistently generating awareness and fostering interest.

Time, talent, and treasure are the three levers that propel action and magnify an organization's impact. Let's look at each of them more closely.

### Time

Time is a precious and often underestimated resource that holds immense potential for driving positive change within mission-driven organizations. When supporters dedicate their time to further a cause, it represents a commitment to the mission and a tangible investment in its success.

Volunteering is a prime example of how individuals can allocate their time to make a meaningful impact. Volunteers offer their skills and expertise to support the organization's programs and initiatives. They become the hands and hearts behind the mission, actively participating in activities that drive change.

Participation in events, whether they are fundraising drives, awareness campaigns, or community outreach programs, is another way individuals contribute their time. Their active involvement not only amplifies the impact of these events but also creates opportunities for them to connect with like-minded individuals who share their passion for the cause.

Advocacy efforts, such as lobbying for policy changes or raising awareness about critical issues, also demand the investment of time. Supporters who engage in advocacy become powerful agents of change, amplifying the organization's voice and influence.

When individuals dedicate their time, they cultivate a sense of ownership and commitment to the cause. They become deeply connected to the mission, forging lasting bonds with the organization and its community.

## Talent

Talent is an invaluable and often untapped resource within mission-driven organizations. Supporters, often possessing diverse skills, experiences, and expertise, offer a wealth of capabilities that can be strategically harnessed to advance the organization's mission. Whether it's expertise in marketing, graphic design, legal matters, organizational management, or any other field, these talent contributions can be transformational.

The range of skills and knowledge that supporters bring to the table can fill crucial gaps within an organization. For instance, a marketing professional can develop and execute effective campaigns to raise awareness and attract new supporters. A talented graphic designer can craft compelling visuals that enhance storytelling and engagement. Legal experts can provide guidance on navigating complex regulatory issues, ensuring the organization operates within legal boundaries.

Beyond filling gaps, talent contributions enhance an organization's capacity to create change. Supporters with specialized skills can drive innovation, streamline operations, and elevate the quality of programs and initiatives. Their contributions provide practical solutions and creative insights that propel the mission forward.

Talent contributions foster a sense of collaboration and shared responsibility among supporters. By actively engaging their expertise, individuals become integral members of the mission-driven community, reinforcing the organization's core values and strengthening its impact.

## Treasure

Financial contributions are critical to mission-driven organizations. Among the three pillars of impact—time, talent, and treasure—financial support stands out as the most straightforward and immediately impactful. It's the financial resources provided by supporters that empower organizations to turn vision into reality and drive their missions forward.

These financial contributions serve as the backbone of funding for various projects, initiatives, and campaigns. They enable organizations to undertake critical work, whether it's funding medical research, supporting underserved communities, or advocating for social change. Financial support goes beyond mere monetary transactions; it represents a tangible commitment to the cause.

## The Intersection of Time, Talent, and Treasure

To fully leverage time and talent, organizations must communicate multiple avenues for action. By creating and communicating diverse opportunities for supporters to engage and contribute, organizations build sustainable systems of community growth and engagement. These systems not only strengthen the organization's core but also provide supporters with meaningful ways to connect and make a difference.

Consider the case of the Make-A-Wish Foundation, an organization dedicated to fulfilling the wishes of children facing critical illnesses. One common misconception is that only terminally ill children receive the opportunity to have their wish granted. To dispel this misconception, individuals who support Make-A-Wish can use their time to share their stories and reinforce awareness. They can leverage their talent, such as marketing expertise, to reach new audiences historically untouched by the organization.

By embracing diverse contributions of time, talent, and treasure, organizations like Make-A-Wish create a ripple effect. Supporters become advocates, sharing their stories and experiences, further amplifying awareness and interest. The community grows stronger, united by a shared purpose and passion for the cause.

The social portion of the SPH model, rooted in connection and powered by storytelling and community, offers a transformative blueprint for scaling social impact. The journey begins with the cultivation of awareness, recognizing its foundational role in building connections. Storytelling is the compass that guides organizations toward deeper interest and engagement. As awareness and interest grow, the three Ts of impact—time, talent, and treasure—become activated, propelling the mission forward.

By continuously nurturing awareness, fostering interest, and embracing diverse contributions, mission-driven organizations create robust communities of support. These communities serve as the driving force behind sustained, meaningful impact. It all starts with the seed of connection planted through storytelling, and from there, the possibilities for positive change are endless.

PART

# Partnerships

Partnerships are the driving force of mission-driven organizations. They are the bridges that connect diverse stakeholders, amplify reach and resources, and move that transformed vision into reality. In social impact, partnerships are the cornerstone on which progress is built. Part II delves into the role that partnerships play in the SPH model, emphasizing their importance in cultivating social opportunities, expanding storytelling, and strengthening connections.

## The Three Pillars of Partnerships

Partnerships are not limited to formal business collaborations or contractual agreements. They encompass a broader spectrum of relationships, connections, and alliances that serve a common purpose—advancing a mission-driven cause. These partnerships can be categorized into three fundamental pillars: strategic, collaborative, and community.

## Strategic Partnerships

Strategic partnerships are meticulously crafted alliances that go beyond mere convenience. They are purpose-driven collaborations rooted in shared goals, values, and a commitment to making a meaningful impact on a specific cause or issue.

What distinguishes strategic partnerships is their intent to create a synergy that surpasses what each partner could achieve independently. These collaborations are not arbitrary but are carefully designed to address specific impact objectives. Whether it's launching a joint campaign to address a pressing social issue, cofunding a critical research project, or combining expertise to develop innovative solutions, strategic partnerships are precision instruments for driving change.

These partnerships capitalize on the unique strengths and resources that each partner brings to the table. By pooling their collective assets, which may include financial resources, expertise, networks, and influence, they can amplify their impact exponentially. Strategic partnerships are not about duplication but rather about complementing and augmenting each other's efforts for a common cause.

## Community Partnerships

Community partnerships represent a vital dimension of collaboration for mission-driven organizations. They are characterized by their close engagement with local, regional, or even global communities and individuals who are deeply connected to the cause. Unlike strategic partnerships that often involve organizations with shared goals and resources, community partnerships are grounded in the power of grassroots movements and passionate individuals.

These partnerships bring organizations closer to the heart of the communities they aim to serve. Whether partnering with local nonprofits, grassroots activists, or dedicated individuals, community partnerships are instrumental in building a robust support network. They tap into the local knowledge, expertise, and networks that community members possess.

One of the most remarkable aspects of community partnerships is the sense of shared ownership they foster. When individuals and local organizations actively participate in the mission, they become not just supporters but also advocates and champions. They embody the cause's values, represent its aspirations, and work passionately to effect change at the grassroots level.

## Collaborative Partnerships

Collaborative partnerships are the embodiment of dynamic cooperation and knowledge exchange in mission-driven organizations. They defy traditional boundaries and unite a diverse spectrum of stakeholders, often including competitors, subject matter experts, thought leaders, and influencers. These partnerships are characterized by their openness to innovation, flexibility, and a shared commitment to finding creative solutions to complex challenges.

At the heart of collaborative partnerships lies the spirit of cooperation. Organizations come together with a willingness to pool their knowledge, expertise, and resources for a common cause. The diversity of perspectives and skills within these partnerships sparks innovation by encouraging fresh ideas and unconventional approaches.

Collaborative partnerships thrive in the spirit of cocreation. Together, partners explore new horizons, develop novel solutions, and navigate evolving landscapes. They are agile in responding to emerging issues and are not bound by rigid structures. Instead, they adapt and evolve to meet the evolving needs of the mission and the changing dynamics of the world.

Partnerships are not just an optional addition to the toolkit of mission-driven organizations; they are the fuel that drives transformative change. Partnerships across these three pillars empower organizations to create social impact by leveraging resources, amplifying reach, fostering innovation, building trust, and adapting to change.

## Cultivating Authenticity in Partnerships

Authentic partnerships are the gold standard for mission-driven organizations. Unlike transactional relationships driven solely by mutual gain, authentic partnerships are rooted in a deeper connection—one founded on shared values, mutual respect, and a genuine commitment to a common cause. Cultivating authenticity within partnerships is not just an ideal; it's an essential strategy for organizations seeking to create meaningful and sustainable change.

Cultivating authenticity in partnerships requires deliberate effort and a commitment to nurturing the relationship with a foundation of shared values. Organizations should begin the partnership journey by identifying and aligning their core values and principles. This alignment serves as the North Star, guiding the partnership's direction and ensuring that both parties are committed to a common cause. It's crucial to engage in open discussions about values to ensure clarity and alignment from the very beginning.

Clear expectations are essential for building trust within partnerships. Organizations should define their roles, responsibilities, and goals in writing. This clarity helps prevent misunderstandings and conflicts down the road. By establishing a clear framework, partners can collaborate effectively while minimizing the potential for misunderstandings.

Organizations should actively foster an environment of mutual respect. This includes valuing the unique perspectives and contributions of each partner, regardless of their size or influence. Demonstrating respect for one another's expertise and experiences creates a positive partnership culture.

Effective communication is the backbone of authenticity. Partners should encourage open and honest dialogue throughout the partnership. This includes sharing successes, challenges, concerns, and feedback. Regular communication helps partners stay informed and ensures that any issues can be addressed promptly.

Transparency builds trust within partnerships. Organizations should be transparent about their actions, decisions, and intentions. This includes sharing information about budgets, project progress, and any changes in direction. Transparency fosters accountability and demonstrates a commitment to working collaboratively.

In authentic partnerships, both parties share responsibility for the partnership's success. This shared responsibility extends beyond individual tasks and encompasses a joint commitment to achieving the partnership's goals. When both organizations actively participate and contribute, it reinforces the sense of partnership and collective ownership.

Authentic partnerships should periodically reflect on their impact and effectiveness. This includes evaluating whether the partnership is achieving its intended outcomes and if adjustments are needed. Reflecting on impact helps partners stay aligned with their mission and purpose.

Authentic partnerships are not static; they are an ongoing journey. Organizations must continually nurture and reinforce authenticity throughout the partnership's life cycle. This includes revisiting shared values, adapting to changing circumstances, and maintaining open lines of communication. As organizations navigate the complex landscape of social impact, authenticity remains a guiding principle that drives meaningful change and transformation.

Organizations engaging in authentic partnerships often discover that they are part of a broader partnership ecosystem. This ecosystem encompasses a rich tapestry of collaborators, each bringing unique strengths, resources, and perspectives to the table. In this intricate web of partnerships, mission-driven organizations must navigate a complex landscape that includes traditional nonprofits, forward-thinking corporations, innovative social enterprises, government agencies, and passionate individuals.

The partnership ecosystem is not a monolithic entity; it is dynamic and ever-evolving. As such, organizations need to approach it with strategic thinking and adaptability. Each partnership within the ecosystem may serve a different purpose, from addressing immediate needs to pursuing long-term impact. Understanding the role and potential of each partner is essential for maximizing the collective impact of the ecosystem.

# 3

# How Should
# Partnerships Look?

Historically, social impact partnerships were somewhat one-dimensional. Corporations often provided financial support in exchange for brand visibility, typically in the form of logos on websites, email blasts, and more recently social media posts. These partnerships were transactional, with a focus on corporate social responsibility (CSR) efforts.

However, the landscape of partnerships is rapidly evolving. Expectations are shifting, and partnerships, along with their partners, are undergoing profound transformations. The new era of partnerships is characterized by a deeper connection to the mission and a greater emphasis on mutual value creation.

Individuals are becoming increasingly vital partners in the social impact ecosystem. They seek more meaningful connections with organizations and require additional insights and information to establish a meaningful link to the mission. Engaging individuals as partners goes beyond soliciting donations; it involves nurturing a sense of shared purpose and active participation.

## Corporate Partners

Corporations have undergone a significant transformation in their approach to impact partnerships. No longer content with merely fulfilling CSR obligations, they are now embracing a more holistic and strategic vision of their role in driving change. This shift is driven by a growing awareness that corporate valuations are no longer solely determined by financial metrics; environmental, social, and governance performance is equally influential. Additionally, consumers are expecting corporations to play an oversized role in positively contributing to society.

Through my work in the impact space, I've developed a concept called Double ROI, and it has emerged as a guiding principle for forming evolved corporate partnerships. This term encapsulates the dual goals that corporations aim to achieve through their engagement with mission-driven organizations:

- **Return on investment.** Corporations seek to derive tangible benefits from their association with social impact initiatives. These benefits include enhanced brand reputation, increased customer loyalty, and improved employee engagement. The partnership should align with the corporation's strategic objectives and contribute positively to its bottom line.

- **Return on impact.** Beyond the corporate benefits, there is a heightened emphasis on the actual impact created by the partnership. Corporations are increasingly interested in measuring the tangible and meaningful outcomes of their contributions to social causes. This includes assessing the social, environmental, and community-driven changes that result from their collaboration with mission-driven organizations.

To achieve these dual objectives, corporations are shifting toward more strategic and comprehensive collaborations. They leverage their resources, expertise, and extensive networks to drive social impact effectively. These partnerships extend beyond financial contributions to include shared knowledge, skills, and innovative solutions. By aligning their corporate values and business strategies with social impact goals, corporations are not only contributing to positive change but also reaping the benefits of enhanced brand equity and a more engaged workforce. This evolution in corporate partnerships marks a significant step toward a more socially responsible and sustainable business ecosystem.

## Influencer Partners

Influencer partnerships have become increasingly pivotal when it comes to social impact. These collaborations harness the power of individuals who have not only amassed substantial followings but also have cultivated trust, authority, and authenticity within their online communities. The rise of social media has enabled influencers to occupy a unique space, and mission-driven organizations have come to recognize the profound value these partnerships bring.

At the heart of influencer partnerships is the ability to extend the reach of social impact initiatives. Influencers have succeeded in building dedicated, engaged audiences that turn to them for guidance, inspiration, and entertainment. Their capacity to capture the attention and admiration of thousands, or even millions, of followers makes them potent advocates for causes and organizations seeking to drive change. When influencers lend their voices and platforms to a mission, the ripple effect can be substantial, creating a groundswell of support and participation.

One of the fundamental attributes that underpins the effectiveness of influencer partnerships is authenticity. Authenticity is the currency of social media, and influencers have mastered the art of genuine storytelling. Their content often reflects their personal experiences, challenges, and triumphs, which resonates deeply with their audience. This authenticity engenders trust and a sense of connection, making followers more receptive to the causes and organizations influencers choose to champion.

The symbiotic relationship between influencers and mission-driven organizations goes beyond the transactional. These partnerships are often founded on shared values, vision, and a mutual commitment to driving positive change. As influencers lend their voices to social impact causes, they become not only spokespeople but also advocates, deeply invested in the mission's success. This genuine commitment can be contagious, inspiring their audience to get involved and make a difference.

Influencers also possess an innate ability to evoke emotion through their content. Emotional resonance is an invaluable ingredient for action, because it taps into the empathy, compassion, and shared values of their audience. Whether it's through heartfelt personal stories, compelling narratives, or poignant calls to action, influencers have a knack for stirring emotions that drive their audiences to support causes and organizations.

Influencer partnerships are not confined to a specific medium or platform. They span a spectrum of online spaces, from Instagram and YouTube to TikTok and Twitter. Each platform offers unique opportunities for engagement and storytelling, enabling influencers to tailor their approach to their target audience. The versatility of influencer partnerships enables mission-driven organizations to leverage multiple channels and maximize their impact.

Although influencer partnerships hold significant promise, they also come with their own set of considerations and strategies. Organizations must carefully select influencers whose values align with their mission, ensuring that the partnership remains authentic and credible. Due diligence is essential to verify an influencer's credibility and audience authenticity, safeguarding against potential misrepresentations.

Influencer partnerships thrive on collaboration and cocreation. Organizations should actively involve influencers in the development of campaigns, initiatives, and content. This collaborative approach ensures that the influencer's unique voice and perspective are integrated seamlessly into the campaign, enhancing its authenticity and effectiveness.

Measurement and evaluation are crucial components of influencer partnerships as well. Organizations must establish clear key performance indicators (KPIs) to assess the partnership's impact. Metrics such as engagement rates, reach, conversion rates, and sentiment analysis can provide valuable insights into the partnership's effectiveness. Continuous monitoring and analysis enable organizations to refine their strategies and optimize future influencer collaborations.

In recent years, the influencer landscape has evolved beyond large, high-reach, individual creators to also encompass influencers with smaller followings, often referred to as micro-influencers and nano-influencers. These smaller-scale influencers have more niche, specialized audiences and can offer unique advantages for mission-driven organizations. Although they may have smaller followings, their communities are often highly engaged and deeply passionate about specific interests or causes. There are no rigid definitions for the terms *micro-influencer* and *nano-influencer*, and sometimes people use them interchangeably. Generally speaking, nano-influencers are even smaller than micro-influencers. But if the nano-influencer has just the right follower base or area of expertise, they could be the perfect match for your organization. Collaborating with micro-influencers and nano-influencers can help organizations to tap into these niche audiences and drive targeted impact.

## Synergistic Cause-Based Partners

In recent years, the partnership landscape has witnessed the emergence of synergistic cause-based collaborations that are reshaping the way organizations tackle complex social challenges. These partnerships are founded on the principle that unity is strength, and they bring together organizations with shared missions or complementary approaches to create a more well-rounded and holistic impact.

What sets these partnerships apart is their commitment to addressing social issues comprehensively. Rather than working in isolation, organizations recognize the power of collective action. They pool their resources, expertise, and strategies to develop multifaceted solutions that encompass various aspects of a problem. This approach enables them to tackle the root causes and intricacies of social challenges, leading to more sustainable and lasting change.

## Building Sustainable, Mutually Beneficial, and Impactful Partnerships

In modern partnership building, organizations are presented with a unique opportunity to craft collaborations that are not only sustainable but also mutually beneficial and impactful. These principles guide the creation of partnerships that transcend mere transactions and become initial groundwork for enduring change.

### Shared Values and Mission Alignment

At the heart of any impactful partnership lies a shared set of values and a unified mission. When organizations commit to a common cause and seek to collaborate, their shared values and mission alignment become the foundational pillars of their partnership. This alignment isn't just a formality; it's the essence that infuses the partnership with purpose, authenticity, and unwavering dedication.

Picture this alignment of values and mission as the North Star guiding the partnership's voyage through the complex waters of social impact. It brings an unmistakable sense of purpose, illuminating the path toward a shared vision. This unified sense of purpose isn't just a lofty ideal; it's a practical and powerful force that keeps the collaborative efforts firmly on course.

Authenticity, a cornerstone of successful partnerships, naturally follows. When partners share values and mission, their authenticity shines through. Authenticity, here, means that the partnership is based on transparency, trust, and a genuine commitment to the cause. This authenticity resonates deeply with stakeholders, engendering trust and forging lasting connections.

Trust, the most precious value in the world of social impact, thrives in the fertile soil of shared values and mission alignment. Partnerships that embody these qualities naturally foster trust among stakeholders, be they supporters, donors, or the wider community. Trustworthiness and credibility are essential for garnering support and ensuring that the partnership's initiatives are viewed as not only credible but also truly impactful.

Harmony in action is another natural outcome. Collaboration is most effective when all parties are aligned in their efforts. Partners who share values and mission are more likely to work harmoniously, pulling in the same direction, and leveraging their combined resources, expertise, and networks toward a common objective. This unity enhances efficiency and minimizes the risk of conflicts or misalignment.

Partnerships are about creating meaningful change, and when values and mission are shared, the impact becomes exponentially greater. This synergy results in initiatives that not only drive impact but also have the sustainability to make a difference over the longer run.

These partnerships become magnets for like-minded supporters. Individuals and organizations that align with the partnership's mission are drawn to it. The shared resonance creates a magnetic pull, attracting supporters who are passionate about the cause and eager to contribute their time, talent, and treasures.

And let's not forget the strategic allocation of resources. In many partnerships, there's a pooling of resources, be it financial, human capital, or expertise. When partners share values and mission, these resources are harnessed for initiatives that mirror the core principles of the collaboration. This strategic allocation ensures that resources are optimized for maximum impact.

But perhaps the most enduring quality is resilience. Shared values and mission provide the motivation to overcome obstacles and adapt to changing circumstances. When partners face challenges or external shifts, their shared commitment to the mission becomes the driving force that propels them forward.

Let's consider a nonprofit organization dedicated to environmental conservation, for example. They're facing a challenge in monitoring and protecting a fragile ecosystem, such as a wildlife sanctuary, due to a recent storm destroying all of their equipment. In this scenario, a corporate partner, a leading technology company, steps in to help.

The corporate partner provides cutting-edge surveillance technology, including drones, remote sensors, and data analytics software, to the nonprofit. They also offer training and support to the nonprofit's staff members in operating and maintaining these technologies. With the advanced tools and expertise provided by the corporate partner, the nonprofit can get back to their important work and mission-critical initiatives.

It's the sustained engagement that seals the deal. Partnerships rooted in shared values and mission tend to generate enduring engagement from stakeholders. Supporters and participants are more likely to stay committed over the long term because they feel a profound connection to the cause and believe in the authenticity of the partnership.

## Authentic Storytelling

The new era of partnerships demands more than just formal collaborations; it requires the genuine, heartfelt storytelling that truly resonates with audiences. Authenticity is not merely a buzzword; it's the essence that infuses partnerships with depth, meaning, and a sense of shared purpose.

At the heart of authentic partnerships is the power of storytelling. Stories have a unique ability to captivate, inspire, and connect. When organizations embark on partnerships, they bring not just their resources but also their narratives, experiences, and visions. These narratives should be more than mere marketing spiels; they should be windows into the soul of the organization, revealing its true mission, values, and the impact it aspires to create.

Partnerships should not be shrouded in secrecy or surface-level interactions. Instead, they should be founded on a genuine willingness to share the organization's mission, its journey, and even its challenges. Authenticity doesn't shy away from acknowledging imperfections; it embraces them as part of the human experience.

Partnerships built on authentic storytelling create a deeper connection not only between the collaborating organizations but also with their respective communities. When partners openly share their mission and impact, it resonates with audiences on a profound level. Audiences appreciate organizations that are not afraid to show their vulnerability, admit to setbacks, and openly discuss their strategies for overcoming obstacles.

Authenticity extends beyond words; it permeates actions. Organizations that are truly committed to their mission and values demonstrate their authenticity through what they say and do. They walk the walk, consistently aligning their actions with their narratives. For example, a bookstore chain that cares about reducing adult illiteracy might donate books to facilities that support adult learning and education. It might even offer financial incentives or free books to people who volunteer to teach reading skills at these facilities.

The authenticity of a partnership is often revealed in the way challenges are tackled. When obstacles arise, authentic partners do not hide them or place blame. Instead, they address issues openly, collaborate to find solutions, and share their experiences as part of the journey. This transparency not only strengthens the partnership but also provides valuable insights for others facing similar challenges.

## Measurement and Impact Assessment

In impact partnerships, there has been a pivotal shift toward a commitment to measurement and analytics. No longer are partnerships solely about logos on websites or superficial collaborations; they are about driving real, tangible change. To achieve this, organizations must establish a robust framework for measuring impact, constantly evaluate their progress, and remain adaptable in their strategies.

**Establishing KPIs and Metrics**   One of the foundational steps in creating partnerships driven by measurable impact is the definition of KPIs and metrics. These metrics serve as the compass by which the partnership's success is gauged. They should be specific, measurable, achievable, relevant, and time-bound, ensuring that they provide a clear road map for assessing progress.

Defining KPIs and metrics requires a collaborative effort between partners. Both organizations must agree on what success looks like and how it will be measured. This alignment is crucial because it sets the stage for the entire partnership. Clear, agreed-on metrics prevent ambiguity and misunderstandings down the road.

The choice of KPIs and metrics should be closely tied to the partnership's objectives and mission. For example, if the partnership aims to reduce food waste, relevant metrics might include the percentage reduction in food waste achieved, the number of meals served to vulnerable populations, or the environmental impact of waste reduction.

Once KPIs and metrics are established, organizations must implement a system for data collection and analysis. Accurate and timely data is vital to impact measurement. This system may involve surveys, data tracking tools, or collaboration with external experts. The key is to ensure that data collection is consistent and aligned with the defined metrics.

**Evaluations** Regular evaluation is an essential component of partnerships geared toward measurable impact. Organizations should schedule periodic check-ins to assess progress against the established KPIs. These evaluations provide an opportunity to celebrate successes, identify areas for improvement, and make necessary adjustments to the partnership's strategies.

Evaluations should not be viewed as a one-time event but as an ongoing process. In dynamic partnerships, circumstances can change, and new challenges or opportunities might emerge. Organizations should remain agile in their approach, ready to pivot when needed.

Sharing impact data and results with the public should also be a key aspect of the measurement and reporting process. It not only demonstrates accountability but also engages supporters and donors. Transparency fosters a sense of ownership and shared responsibility for the partnership's success.

In addition to internal evaluations, external assessments by third-party experts can provide valuable insights into the partnership's impact. Independent evaluations add credibility to the partnership's claims and offer an unbiased perspective on its effectiveness.

**Sustainability and Adaptability** Partnerships should also consider the long-term sustainability of their impact. Although short-term gains are important, the ultimate goal is to create lasting change. Partners should explore strategies to ensure that their impact continues beyond the duration of the partnership. In pursuing this goal, they should keep in mind that long-term sustainability sometimes requires a certain amount of adaptability.

Collaboration on impact measurement can extend beyond the partnership itself. Partners can engage with other organizations, research institutions, or government agencies to share data, research findings, and best practices. Such collaborations contribute to a broader understanding of the partnership's impact and promote knowledge sharing.

In the chapters that follow, we will delve deeper into the various forms that partnerships can take within this evolving landscape. From strategic alliances and community collaborations to innovative cross-sector partnerships, we will explore how organizations can leverage different types of partnerships to advance their missions and create positive social change.

# 4

# Whom Should
# You Partner Up With?

We are now very clear about what a partnership should look like, so let's start looking at whom you should consider partnering up with. There are right and wrong ways to go about a new partnership, and you may need to make some tough choices along the way. With this in mind, let's have a look at the kinds of partnerships that you might get into, including the kinds of partnerships that you should avoid depending on what kind of organization you are.

## Speaking the Partnership Language

In Chapter 3, we made it clear that a partnership should have shared views, values, and similar or aligned goals. That being said, we need to break this down further. The partnerships you enter should be made on the basis of three core ideas: collaboration, mutual gains, and a consideration for each other's interests. Before you agree to collaborate with another person or organization, take some time to think about these three important concepts.

First, there is *collaboration*. When you think of the person or organization that you are discussing a partnership with, do you feel that you can be great collaborators? Now, you may be thinking, How can I know before I actually start working with them? There are cues that can be picked up before you agree. For example, you might want to ask yourself whether the potential partner is respectful of your time. Is there any direct connection to your mission? Or, are they more interested in talking about their own organization and what you can do for them? Collaboration can involve sharing resources and expertise and can take place with individuals, organizations, or groups, but the key word here is *with*. Collaboration is not a one-way street. Collaboration can be an effective way to solve complex problems, generate new ideas, and achieve success that would not be possible working alone.

Second, there needs to be *mutual gains*. The collaborative work should center on building awareness, fostering interest, and generating actions in the partnership and the mission. Ideally, the collaboration would be measured and quantified so that optimization decisions can be made, creating more effective impact across these various awareness, interest, and action tactics.

Third, you have to ensure that you are considerate of the other's interests as well. Sometimes, especially as a cause-based organization, you may start looking around for a new partner with great intentions of boosting your organization's success and social impact. It's easy to look at every opportunity in front of you as a great one, but this is the wrong way to approach it. Instead, look at how the other might benefit from your partnerships. Make sure to highlight this, show that you are interested in helping them get there, and that their goals are aligned both with your why as well as your goals. For example, an organization that wants to improve women's wages in the workplace might partner with an organization that is encouraging the participation of girls in STEM programs in schools. Or a health care organization looking to reduce their garbage and waste footprint might partner with an organization that specializes in consulting and certifying businesses in their facilities' management and waste processes.

Speaking the partnership language means that you should be focusing on collaborating with others. It means to understand and use the terminology, concepts, and frameworks that are commonly used in partnerships and collaboration, and to internalize these into your everyday work whenever you seek to create relationships with partners and others who come onto your team (e.g., collaborating, mutual gains, and so on). This can include understanding the different types of partnerships and their goals, the roles and responsibilities of each partner, and applying each of these to the partnerships you get into. However, it also means knowing how to spot a potentially harmful partnership.

## Partner Discernment

As mentioned, whenever we start a new project, we tend to be very excited and might end up feeling like any new partner is a good idea if it means that we are likely to gain exposure, credibility, and value. However, this perspective might not be the right one to take, namely because you could end up partnering up with the wrong organizations. The wrong partner could be a drain on resources, block the right opportunities, or hurt your brand. So it's important to not only research but have some internal agreement on what the make up of an ideal partner is by using a framework from what has been outlined in this chapter.

Let's think about the following scenario. The organization we are running is one that aims to alleviate poverty in a small community in Wyoming. It is trying to do so by providing upskilling opportunities through courses, scholarships, workshops, and by bringing start-up project heads to different areas of the state. The organization, ScaleUpWyoming, is looking to accomplish its goals within the next few years and so far has worked primarily through donations. Now, however, it is running out of funds and has been furiously looking for more funding. Donations are running dry because the cost of living is increasing tremendously and people are now tending to save more as opposed to spend more. While pushing content out on their Instagram page, they receive a direct message from a venture capital firm proposing a meeting to discuss a potential partnership. At first, the head of the organization is, of course, thrilled—will this be the way out of this financial issue?

After taking some time to think about this potential partnership, the head of ScaleUpWyoming, Alex, decides to do some research. The venture capital firm at first seems interesting, but after digging a bit more, she realizes that their accreditation and licenses seem a bit dodgy. She looks at their social media accounts and again finds that it seems a bit unserious. Then, looking online again and searching through the news, she finds that the firm has actually been involved in numerous data scandals where they allowed the sale of their clients' data. Naturally, as the people Alex's organization works with are already vulnerable, working with a firm that is known for performing illegal actions is not a good look. Alex mentions this to them, and they explain that they are teaming up with organizations like hers to polish up their image, something that Alex had thought of. Should Alex work with them? What if it means ruining the organization's reputation? And, what if it means that the organization stops working altogether if she doesn't get their cash infusion?

The answers to these questions are quite hard to establish, mainly because they depend on the values that you hold as an organization. Do you value your organization's survival over the potential risk to your reputation that the partnership may have? Or do you perhaps value the ethics and morals of the organization above all? These are decisions that you need to make before you start choosing your partners. That being said, when choosing whom to partner with, you need to consider how this partnership is likely to make your organization look once this partnership is out in the open. Ultimately, if the potential partnership has a commitment to transparency, aligned vision and values, and is synergistic, then it is likely a workable and impactful partnership. This could be a corporate partner, an individual, another nonprofit, or even a social media influencer.

CHAPTER

# 5

# Partnering
# with Influencers

S o far, we have established that leveraging social media is a
crucial aspect of your approach as an organization trying to
have a significant social impact. Having said that, there is a limit
to how much you can leverage social media without working
with partners. The most effective and impactful partners on
social media are influencers.

Influencers are individuals who have the power to influence
the actions and decisions of others because of their authority,
knowledge, position, or relationship with their audience. Social
media influencers are often used by companies to promote their
products or services to a wide audience because they have a large
following on social media platforms and can effectively reach
many people. Although the job of being an influencer was initially
somewhat misunderstood, over the past few years, its
understanding has changed along with the potential value of

these influencers. Influencers used to be seen as people who simply put a camera up in their face and danced around on TikTok; they are now seen as true businesses, especially in a world where they tend to have a significant amount of power over what people do.

## How Do Influencers Help?

As mentioned, influencers can help you in a few ways. First, they can bring much more awareness to a cause. By working with them, you are tapping into the power of their social media accounts, including the engagement tactics they can use (e.g., commenting, liking, sharing your content).

Second, you can also reach new audiences and raise awareness surrounding your mission, cause, or your organization. Influencers can have a large and engaged audience, so partnering with them can help to increase the visibility of your organization and reach a wider audience than you might be able to on your own. This is especially true in regards to the limits that traditional social media tactics have (e.g., character limitations, organic reach, and Google's ability to crawl social media accounts for SEO), because sometimes, even following all the rules for content and being algorithm-friendly still will not work!

Influencers also are trusted by their followers, so partnering with them can help improve your credibility and trustworthiness in the eyes of your current or desired audience. With credibility and trustworthiness comes community and a sense of loyalty as well, which is something that influencers can help you build (because they often have a strong connection with their audience and can encourage their followers to support your brand).

Influencer marketing has also been shown to be an effective and cost-efficient way to reach your target audience without needing a large marketing investment and can result in a higher return compared to other forms of advertising (e.g., pay-per-click and other forms of paid ads).

Finally, working with influencers can provide valuable insights into your target audience, including their preferences, behaviors, and pain points, which can help you create more effective marketing campaigns and communication tactics.

## Different Kinds of Influencers

Everyone has a certain degree of influence, no matter the size of their following. Even if your social media audience consists of 20 followers, your recommendations and endorsements can carry weight.

If you make a book or movie recommendation to your 20 followers, you will likely sway some of your followers to check that book or movie out. Let's explore the fascinating spectrum of influencers, from the major players with millions of followers to the smaller, yet impactful, influencers with more limited but engaged audiences.

Major influencers are the heavyweights of the social media world. These individuals have amassed vast followings, often numbering in the millions. Their reach is extensive, and their content can sway and inspire countless individuals. Major influencers typically have a far-reaching impact and can affect trends and discussions on a global scale. If a major influencer endorses a product or supports a cause, it can lead to a significant boost in visibility and engagement.

On the other end of the spectrum, we have smaller influencers, often with 10 to 50,000 followers. Although their reach may not be as expansive as that of major influencers, their influence is no less potent. Their audiences trust their opinions and are more likely to engage with their content. Collaborating with smaller influencers can be incredibly effective when seeking to connect with specific demographics or interest groups.

Mid-level influencers occupy a sweet spot, with follower counts ranging between 50,000 to 100,000. These influencers offer a balance between reach and engagement. They have cultivated substantial followings, yet their audiences remain highly engaged and interactive. Mid-level influencers often strike a chord with their followers by delivering content that resonates deeply with their interests and values.

Although follower count is a noteworthy factor, the true measure of an influencer's impact lies in their engagement rate. Engagement encompasses various interactions on social media, such as likes, comments, shares, and more. High engagement indicates that a piece of content has struck a chord with the audience, making it more visible and influential. Algorithms on social media platforms appreciate high engagement because it keeps users on the platform longer. For influencers, this robust engagement signifies trust and influence over their followers.

When partnering with influencers, it's crucial to consider not only their follower count but also the level of engagement they receive. An influencer with a smaller following but high engagement may yield better results in terms of authentic connections and meaningful impact. The trust they've cultivated with their audience can translate into genuine support for your cause.

Influence on social media is not solely determined by the number of followers one has. Instead, it's a multifaceted concept that encompasses the ability to engage and inspire an audience authentically. Whether you collaborate with major influencers, smaller niche creators, or mid-level experts, the key lies in aligning their influence with your mission and values. By doing so, you can leverage their impact to create meaningful connections and drive positive change.

# Choosing the Right Influencer

Choosing the right influencer to partner with is one of the most important steps you can take for your organization. You want to be able to find someone who has the right personality, the right content, and, most important, alignment in values and vision. Choosing an influencer, or influencers, to partner with is a big decision and not one that should be taken lightly. If done correctly, these partnerships can help increase awareness, interest, engagement, and activation from their audience—building the framework for a repeatable, scalable, and sustainable program.

There are a number of different types of influencers. They range from industry experts and celebrities to bloggers, journalists, and entrepreneurs. Each type has its advantages and disadvantages. Some may be better suited for your organization's goals than others, so you need to ensure that their content, messaging, personality, and values are in line with your own. In addition to assessing the influencer's content and audience in terms of their viability as a partner, you should also check for any sponsored posts. You don't want to choose an influencer who has a huge following but doesn't identify sponsored posts in a way that conforms with laws and regulations; their behavior reflects on you; These are all important factors, but how do you go about weighing influencers to see if they're right for you? Let's look at some qualities and traits you can consider.

## Authenticity

Authenticity not only ensures genuine engagement but also enhances the overall performance of your campaign. It can lay the foundation for long-term, meaningful relationships with both the influencer and their audience.

When seeking influencer partnerships, authenticity should be non-negotiable. Authentic influencers are those whose values, interests, and content align organically with your cause. These individuals are not merely endorsing a product or a message for financial gain but are genuinely passionate and knowledgeable about the subject matter.

Authenticity is a two-fold requirement. First, it means finding influencers whose personal beliefs and interests genuinely align with your organization's mission. For example, if your organization advocates for environmental sustainability, partnering with influencers who are passionate environmentalists will naturally foster authenticity.

Second, authenticity extends to the influencer's relationship with their audience. Authentic influencers have cultivated trust and credibility among their followers. They have built these connections through transparent and honest interactions, sharing personal experiences, and demonstrating a sincere commitment to their chosen niche.

When an influencer authentically aligns with your message or product, their endorsement carries more weight. Their audience recognizes this alignment and is more likely to engage with the content and, ultimately, take action. Authenticity breeds trust, and trust fuels influence.

In the long run, authenticity in influencer partnerships can lead to enduring relationships. When influencers genuinely support your cause or product, they are more likely to continue collaborating with your organization. These ongoing partnerships can deepen the impact of your campaigns, because they are built on a foundation of mutual trust and shared values.

## Reputation

Reputation plays a pivotal role in selecting the right influencer partner for your campaign. An influencer's reputation serves as a reflection of their credibility and the trust they have built with their audience. When partnering with influencers, it's crucial to consider their reputation in terms of their personal brand and their expertise in relevant subject matters.

A strong influencer partner should possess a positive personal reputation. They should be well-regarded by their followers for their authenticity, honesty, and consistency. A respected influencer is one who consistently delivers valuable content and engages with their audience in an ethical and transparent way. Their positive reputation can serve as a bridge to building trust with your organization's target audience.

An influencer's ability to speak persuasively on topics related to your organization is also important. For example, if your organization focuses on protecting vulnerable communities from climate change, partnering with an influencer renowned for their commitment to veganism and a zero-waste lifestyle aligns perfectly. Such an influencer not only embodies the values associated with environmental conservation but also possesses the knowledge and credibility to discuss climate-related issues convincingly.

An influencer's reputation extends beyond their follower count. It encompasses their track record of advocating for causes, their consistency in delivering messages that resonate with your mission, and their ability to drive meaningful conversations within their niche. A strong influencer partner leverages their reputation to effectively convey your organization's message, making it more relatable and compelling to their audience.

## Aligning with Your Goals

Keep your goals in mind. Your objectives will guide you in choosing the type of influencer who best aligns with your campaign's specific goals.

One approach is to collaborate with macro-influencers or celebrities who boast large followings. These individuals can provide your campaign with massive reach. With their extensive reach, macro-influencers can expose your message to a vast and diverse audience quickly. If your primary goal is to raise general awareness or reach a broad demographic, partnering with macro-influencers might be the right strategy.

However, it's equally crucial to consider the potential of micro-influencers and nano-influencers. These influencers may have smaller but highly engaged audiences within specific niches or communities. Their followers trust their recommendations and opinions, leading to higher levels of engagement and authentic interactions. If your campaign aims to generate deeper interest, foster meaningful engagement, or drive specific actions within a niche audience, micro-influencers and nano-influencers can be incredibly effective.

Ultimately, the choice between partnering with macro-, micro-, or nano-influencers depends on your campaign objectives. It's not a one-size-fits-all approach; instead, it should align with your specific goals. Assess the reach and engagement potential of each influencer category and determine which one best serves your campaign's purpose. By keeping your goals in mind and strategically selecting influencers accordingly, you can maximize the impact and effectiveness of your influencer marketing efforts.

With this in mind, we are now ready to head into Chapter 6, where we will be exploring how you can create such partnerships.

CHAPTER

# 6

# How to Grow Partnerships

Now that we know the people you will want to grow partnerships with, let's explore *how* you can grow these partnerships. Oftentimes, growing partnerships can feel like it is a very exhausting task because of the amount of work that appears to be needed to foster these relationships. However, this is not necessarily the case. In reality, your organization can efficiently foster growth by employing the right strategies and adopting a well-considered approach. This chapter will serve as your guide, unveiling the pathways to partnership expansion and outlining the strategies that can facilitate this journey. Together, we'll discover that the road to partnership growth is paved with potential, and, with the right tools, it can become a transformative experience for your organization's mission-driven goals.

# The Three Ts of Partnership

In mission-centered work, partnerships are the engine that drives progress. They are the conduits through which an organization's impact can flow, whether it's through the contributions of individual volunteers, the expertise of talented collaborators, or the financial support of donors and corporate allies. To truly grasp the essence of partnership value, we must delve into the three Ts—time, talent, and treasure—as first discussed in Chapter 2.

These three pillars sustain every partnership, regardless of its scale or nature. Whether engaging with individual volunteers, influencers, or corporate entities, understanding how these resources are harnessed on both sides of the partnership equation is crucial for fostering meaningful connections.

## Time

Volunteers who generously invest their time in your cause bring with them a wealth of dedication and energy. Their commitment can extend far beyond the mere hours they contribute. It can manifest as a passion that ignites your mission, inspires others, and cultivates a sense of shared ownership. The dimension of time also holds the potential for creating profound social moments that organically amplify your mission.

When individuals invest their time, they become emotionally intertwined with your mission, forging a deep and lasting connection. This emotional connection is the foundation of social moments, those transformative instances when people come together to share their passion and purpose.

Volunteers often extend their commitment beyond the clock. Their dedication transcends their volunteer hours, spilling over into their everyday lives. They become your mission's storytellers, weaving narratives of their experiences and spreading the word to their friends, family, professional networks, and social circles. These organic advocates breathe life into your cause, sparking conversations and igniting curiosity.

Volunteers also inspire others by their example. Their visible devotion serves as a compelling testament to the power of your mission. People witnessing this dedication are more likely to consider lending their own time, and ultimately talents, or treasure to your cause.

This ripple effect transforms isolated acts of kindness into a wave of collective impact. It showcases the synergy of partnerships, where the investment of time leads to a cascade of social moments that propel your mission forward. As the stories of volunteers' commitment spread, they create opportunities for others to join, share, and participate in the journey.

In essence, time is not just a resource; it's the entry point for engagement and connection. It creates a dynamic ecosystem of shared moments, when your mission becomes a shared experience. The social moments generated by the investment of time help your mission resonate far and wide, drawing more partners into your impact community.

## Talent

Collaborators who bring unique skills, experiences, and expertise to the table enhance your organization's capacity to create meaningful change. It's not just about having access to talent; it's about leveraging it effectively to address complex challenges and innovate solutions.

Talent can lead your organization and your mission into meaningful transformation and innovation. Collaborators with specialized skills can help your organization navigate intricate challenges and devise creative solutions. Their diverse perspectives can shed new light on longstanding issues, leading to breakthroughs that might have otherwise remained elusive.

But the true magic of talent in partnerships lies in its potential to spark innovation. It's not just about the skills an individual or organization brings but how those skills can be creatively harnessed to drive your mission forward. These talents often intersect with your own, creating a dynamic fusion of abilities that can yield groundbreaking results.

Partnerships built on talent foster a culture of continuous learning and growth. They provide opportunities for knowledge exchange and skill development, enriching both sides of the collaboration. These collaborative learning experiences amplify the impact of talent, as partners mutually benefit from the exchange of expertise. Talent, when effectively channeled, becomes a place for creativity and transformation, enriching your mission with brilliance and purpose.

### Treasure

Traditionally, treasure in the form of financial support has taken center stage in the partnership narrative. Although undoubtedly vital, treasure should not overshadow the significance of time and talent. In fact, the real power of partnerships often lies in harnessing all three of these elements in harmony.

Financial contributions foundationally powers mission-driven organizations. They fuel initiatives, empower projects, and drive impact. However, it's essential to recognize that financial support is not a one-way transaction; it's a reciprocal relationship.

Treasure represents more than currency; it symbolizes trust and commitment. Donors and partners invest their resources with the expectation of a return—a return measured not in monetary terms but in the tangible difference their support can make in the world. This expectation is rooted in a shared vision and a belief that their treasure can support real transformation.

Financial support is a dynamic exchange. Donors and partners entrust their treasure to your organization because they see the potential for their investment to align with their values and aspirations. They envision their contributions as seeds that will grow to facilitate positive change.

Treasure-driven partnerships emphasize accountability and transparency. It's about stewarding resources with care, ensuring that every dollar invested serves the mission's purpose and contributes to the envisioned impact. This collaborative approach fosters a sense of shared responsibility, where both parties actively engage in the journey toward a brighter future.

Treasure within the context of partnerships is also a source of empowerment. It provides the means to scale initiatives, reach underserved communities, and amplify the mission's reach. Financial contributions can fuel innovation, enabling organizations to tackle complex challenges and seize opportunities that might otherwise remain out of reach.

Ultimately, the dimension of treasure in partnerships embodies the transformative potential of collective action. It exemplifies the profound impact that can be achieved when like-minded individuals and organizations come together, pooling their resources, trust, and commitment to drive positive change.

## The Three Ts Work Together

The beauty of the three Ts lies in their interdependence. Time, talent, and treasure are not isolated elements but interconnected forces that can amplify each other when orchestrated effectively. A volunteer's time and talent can magnify their financial contributions, just as a corporate partner's treasure can enhance the impact of their employees' volunteered time and expertise.

As you navigate the world of partnerships, remember that each T has its unique role to play. Embrace the diversity and depth that each partner brings to the table, and seek to unlock the full potential of the three Ts in every collaboration. By doing so, you'll discover that partnerships are not merely about transactions but transformative journeys that empower your organization to reach new heights of impact and purpose.

## Help Others So They Want to Help You

A mutually beneficial partnership is one in which both organizations—you and your partner—can achieve their goals and objectives through the partnership. This means that both of you should be able to see a clear benefit from the partnership and be willing to invest time and resources into making it a success. For example, if your organization is partnering with a corporation, you should be able to showcase how the partnership will accelerate your mission, as well as communicate the value the partnership also brings to their corporation. That being said, this is also similar when it comes to creating any mission-oriented partnership, including influencers or even other nonprofits. When you propose this partnership, you need to make sure that you are being very clear about the benefits that your partnership is going to bring for all parties involved. The most successful, long-term partnerships will be ones where there is mutual benefit.

Likewise, you will want to make sure that you are communicating clearly. Clear communication and transparency are crucial in creating a mutually beneficial partnership between your organization and the individual or party whom you would like to work with. Both parties should have a clear understanding of each other's goals, objectives, and expectations. For example, are you looking to work with an influencer to increase your organization's visibility? If so, what is the influencer gaining from this experience? Does this partnership help bring them further validation to their audience? It's also important to establish clear lines of communication and make sure that everyone involved in the partnership—which might also involve other people, such as the influencer's manager—understands their roles and responsibilities so the partnership can run as effectively as possible. Regular meetings and progress updates can help ensure that everyone is on the same page and can help ensure that no one falls behind or feels lost in the process. A partnership needs to have everyone on board, communicating candidly, and transparently sharing as much as possible.

When it comes to making sure that your team feels like you are both benefiting from this, you need to keep in mind that you should stay as flexible as possible. Partnerships often involve different organizations with different priorities and ways of working. It is very rare that we are able to figure out ways to work with people and organizations that do things exactly as you do. Being open to new ideas and perspectives, and being willing to adjust the partnership as needed to meet the evolving needs of all parties involved, is something that every good partnership needs—and it is something that you need to be able to do yourself if you want your partnerships to be sustainable and to work in the long run.

## It's About Using Each Party's Strengths

Both parties should also leverage each other's strengths; for example, what can you do that the partner needs help with? What can your partner do that you may need help with? In impact work, this is usually looked at through the lens of some financial transaction. However, it's important to not forget the strategic aspects of your partners. Your organization should leverage the strengths of your partners to achieve your goals, whether this is something like marketing or even just getting their advice based on the experience that they have. For example, the influencer you are working with may have expertise in a particular area (e.g., marketing), and you may have a strong network of supporters who can help the influencer build an audience that aligns better with their values. By working together, you can achieve more than you could on your own.

Focusing on each other's strengths is also a great way for you to make sure that you are sharing the same vision. As partners, being on the same page and being focused on achieving the same goals is very important. You need to know that you are working toward a shared goal, and a great way to do this is by seeing how you can use one another's strengths to support and overcome your weaknesses. Think about what help you may need and, in turn, what kind of help you could bring to the table. Remember that being a mission-driven organization is an asset and that your partners want to be associated with your platform.

## Pitching Your Partnership

It's imperative to position your organization as an attractive and valuable collaborator. The days of simple logo promotion are evolving into a more sophisticated era where partnerships are built on mutual value, shared goals, and a commitment to elevating impact and mission success. To effectively engage potential partners, you must move beyond traditional approaches and embrace the art of persuasive partnership pitching.

One of the core principles of successful partnership pitching is the cultivation of mutually desired outcomes. It's about aligning the objectives and aspirations of both parties to create a win-win scenario that amplifies the impact of each partner. You're crafting a narrative in which collaboration becomes the reason for achieving more substantial and meaningful results.

Think of it as painting a vivid picture of the future—a future where the partnership becomes a guiding example for achieving shared success. What will your organization gain? What will your potential partner achieve? Why should they choose to collaborate with you on this journey? Your pitch should be so convincing that it resonates with your own conviction.

Injecting empathy, authenticity, and a genuine commitment to meeting your partner's expectations is pivotal. Partnerships are built on trust, and trust is fostered when both parties feel heard, valued, and understood. Approach potential partners as individuals, not entities, and seek to forge connections that extend beyond the transactional.

## Prioritize the Right People

Though it may seem that there is an endless supply of potential partnerships, prioritization is a crucial step to ensure that your resources are invested wisely and your goals are effectively met. Not all partnerships are created equal, and it's essential to identify and engage with those who align with your mission and can contribute significantly to your objectives.

First and foremost, it's important to recognize that it's neither feasible nor advisable to partner with everyone. Attempting to form partnerships indiscriminately can lead to dilution of focus, resources, and efforts. Instead, adopt a strategic approach by carefully selecting partners whose interests align with your own, whose involvement can result in tangible benefits, and through collaboration can help achieve exponential outcomes.

As you embark on this journey, consider your short-term aspirations and long-term goals. What specific outcomes are you aiming to achieve through partnerships? Whether it's raising awareness, expanding your reach, securing funding, or enhancing your impact, your partnership strategy should be tailored to support these objectives.

The fundamental criteria for prioritizing partnerships is alignment. Partnerships that thrive are those in which the interests, values, and missions of both organizations converge. Seek out partners whose vision harmonizes with yours because this synergy forms the foundation for meaningful collaboration.

Another vital aspect of partner selection is identifying complementary strengths. Although it's essential to acknowledge your organization's capabilities and weaknesses, it's equally crucial to recognize the expertise, resources, and assets that potential partners bring to the table. Partnerships should be symbiotic, with each party contributing unique strengths to address shared challenges effectively.

Additionally, assess the capacity of potential partners to help you reach your goals. Do they possess the right resources, knowledge, and experience to make a substantial impact? The wrong partner, one lacking the necessary alignment, can become a drain on your organization's people, time, and resources, hindering your ability to cultivate meaningful collaborations in the long run.

Remember that the process of forming partnerships is not one-size-fits-all. Each partnership should be tailored to serve specific purposes and objectives, whether they are focused on immediate needs or long-term strategic goals. By being selective and prioritizing partners who align with your mission, bring complementary strengths, and possess the capacity to make a substantial difference, you can optimize the impact of your collaborative efforts.

By asking critical questions, evaluating alignment, and assessing strengths and capacity, you can identify partners who will contribute significantly to your mission and help you achieve your goals more effectively. Quality partnerships, rooted in shared values and mutual benefit, have the potential to amplify your impact and drive positive change in your community and beyond.

## Cultivate—Don't Compete

Similar to any relationship, effective communication is the hallmark a of successful partnership. It's the bridge that connects organizations, aligns efforts, and ensures everyone involved understands their roles and responsibilities. To cultivate a thriving partnership, clear and open lines of communication must be established and maintained.

At the onset of establishing clear communication, it's also important to clarify roles and responsibilities. It's essential that every stakeholder in the partnership understands their specific duties and contributions. By clearly defining these roles, you avoid overlap and ensure that everyone is working efficiently toward the shared goal.

In addition to role clarity, it's crucial to address any concerns or reservations openly. Partnerships often involve multiple organizations with distinct cultures, practices, and priorities so it's not uncommon for questions or doubts to arise along the way. Encourage a culture of open dialogue through which partners can express their thoughts, challenges, or ideas without fear of judgment. These conversations can lead to constructive solutions, build trust, and strengthen the partnership. For example, maybe a real estate developer wants to invest in an area of a city, while the local historical society wants to preserve the existing building facades. The two groups have reasons to initially distrust each other, but working together, they might get special tax breaks, grants, and bonds that would enable them to restore and retain the facades of the buildings while updating the interiors.

Regular meetings and progress updates serve as vital touchpoints for maintaining alignment. They provide an opportunity to review achievements, discuss challenges, and adapt strategies as needed. Although these meetings might at times seem tedious or time-consuming, they are an essential investment in the health of the partnership. They help ensure that everyone remains on the same page and that the partnership continues to meet the evolving needs and expectations of everyone involved.

It's also essential to set aside ego and competition in favor of collaboration. Partnerships are not a place for organizations to compete for the spotlight or individual recognition. Instead, they are vehicles for collective progress, where the success of one partner contributes to the success of all. The old saying "A rising tide lifts all boats" illustrates the value of collaboration perfectly. By working together toward a common goal, organizations can achieve more significant impact than they could individually.

## Know When to Step Away

A partnership, whether in your personal or professional life, should be a source of excitement and growth. It should enrich your organization, bringing value, resources, and shared goals. However, just as in a romantic relationship, it's crucial to recognize when a partnership is no longer serving its purpose and may even be detrimental to your mission.

You should never feel compelled to remain in a partnership that drains your organization's time, resources, and energy without offering substantial returns. Just as in any relationship, if the partnership doesn't contribute positively to your mission, it may be time to reevaluate and consider whether it's the right fit. Remember, a partnership should be an investment with clear and mutual benefits. If this is not the case, it's perfectly acceptable to question its value and viability.

Although it may sound counterintuitive, considering how to gracefully exit a partnership if needed is a sign of strategic thinking. It acknowledges that partnerships carry inherent risks, and having contingency plans in place demonstrates your organization's commitment to its mission and objectives.

Growing a partnership hinges on ensuring that all parties involved feel valued and appreciated. It's a reciprocal relationship built on trust, shared vision, and effective communication. Your goals and those of your partner should align seamlessly, and both parties should be unwaveringly dedicated to the cause you're championing. Success in partnerships requires a readiness to listen, engage, and fulfill your commitments—a true team effort.

Reflecting on the previous chapters, we've explored various facets of partnerships: how to identify potential partners, whom to consider partnering with, and strategies for nurturing these partnerships. Armed with this knowledge, we are now prepared to jump into Chapter 7, a journey into the art of connecting humanity to mission and the cultivation of genuine human connections.

# Human

As we conclude this model, we bring the focus back to the fundamental essence of all social impact work: humanity. Throughout the SPH model, it becomes evident that at its core, this work is based on connecting with people, understanding their needs, and striving to make a positive difference in their lives. It's a journey that entails building relationships, ensuring others feel heard and valued, and fostering partnerships that result in meaningful change for individuals and communities. In philanthropy and social impact, the ultimate goal is to better the human experience, and this intention lies at the center of everything we do.

In this final part of the book, we delve into the concept of being human. We explore the intricacies of creating and nurturing connections, examining the art of empathy, and unraveling the mysteries of amplifying impact. This is where we learn to distinguish between actions that genuinely do good and those that may inadvertently harm progress. The human aspects of social impact work ensures that your organization is not only set up for success but also primed to deliver the maximum possible impact.

Part III will cover all things human to ensure that your organization is set up to deliver the most possible impact. Real people, with real lives, making real sacrifices, run real organizations. Understanding the human dimension of social impact work is not just beneficial but also essential.

We will navigate the nuances of human connections, explore the power of empathy in fostering understanding and collaboration, and unravel the intricacies of multiplying impact to create a better world for all. The human element, with its complexities and subtleties, is central to every aspect of our work, and it's what makes this journey challenging and profoundly rewarding.

Throughout this model, we've explored strategies, principles, and frameworks aimed at helping you navigate the diverse social impact landscape. However, these tools and insights are most impactful when applied within the context of genuine human interactions and relationships. Ultimately, the success of your organization's mission relies on the meaningful connections you forge, the empathy you extend, and the positive impact you create for the individuals and communities you serve. The human side of social impact honors the spirit of humanity and its potential to effect profound transformations.

# 7

# Creating and Nurturing Connections

According to Maslow's hierarchy of needs, connection and belonging is considered a basic human need. It is considered a psychological need and is placed in the third level of the hierarchy, which also includes the need for safety and security. Maslow believed that individuals cannot reach their full potential and self-actualization unless their basic needs are met. We crave connection because it helps us feel more comfortable, safer, and like we have a social circle to fall back on if things were to go wrong.

As humans, we are social creatures. We have a natural inclination to seek out and form connections with others. From an evolutionary perspective, this makes total sense. Early humans needed to rely on others for survival. For example, they needed to work together to hunt for food, protect themselves from predators, and raise children. Doing this on one's own was practically impossible in a time where one could be eaten by a tiger at night—perhaps an extreme example, but you get the point. This need for connection and belonging has only intensified as human societies have grown more complex and communities have become larger. Though our societies have become increasingly individualist in some ways, we have also become more reliant on one another for other reasons. There are no longer tigers roaming around to eat us at night, in most places, but we rely on people to bring us our food through global food chains. Most communities are no longer raising all of the children collectively, and often people hire babysitters or other childcare services. So to say that we are more individualistic than before may not be an accurate depiction of where we truly are.

In fact, connection with others is essential for physical and mental well-being. Studies have shown that social connections can have a positive impact on physical health, helping to lower blood pressure, reduce stress, and improve overall cardiovascular health.[1] Being closely connected to people can also have a positive impact on our mental health and emotional well-being, namely because it makes us feel like we do not have to worry about being alone—we feel supported and that there are people who are willing to help us. This is applicable to many other parts of our society, including that of philanthropic organizations.

This need for connection and belonging can manifest in different ways within our personal and professional lives. For example, for you, it may be the desire to have close relationships with a small group of people, such as family and friends. For others, it may be the desire to be part of a larger community, such as a religious group or a sports team. You might know this as well if your organization works directly with people because you are likely seeing how they need or rely on a community or a support system. Indeed, as humans, we have a fundamental need

---

[1]https://www.ncbi.nlm.nih.gov/pmc/articles/PMC3150158/

for being loved, accepted, and respected by others, and this is a need that you need to acknowledge as an organization.

## How Can I Create Connections?

Creating and nurturing connections is the soul of social impact work. These connections extend beyond the partnerships and collaborations between organizations; they encompass the relationships formed by individuals within and outside these organizations. Understanding where and how to forge these connections is essential for growing your mission and fostering a sense of community.

Previously in this book, we emphasized the importance of creating social moments, both online and offline, as a means to cultivate a vibrant community and strengthen connections. These moments spur human interaction, providing opportunities for people to come together, share their experiences, and engage with your mission. However, the value of these connections extends far beyond these moments; they lay the foundation for lasting relationships that can significantly affect your organization's effectiveness.

We can sometimes lose sight of the profound significance of human connection, particularly when focusing on the mission's beneficiaries. However, it's equally crucial to recognize the humanity within the individuals who work tirelessly to create and deliver this impact. As we look toward a future where we fully acknowledge and appreciate the humanity behind every mission, it becomes imperative to support one another's efforts, acknowledge the work being done, and create a sustainable environment for real people to drive real change.

This recognition extends to your partners as well. In mission-driven work, or any work for that matter, it's easy for interactions to become transactional. However, it's essential never to lose sight of the humanity that connects every aspect of impact delivery. Partnerships, collaborations, and alliances might involve formal agreements and strategic goals, but at their core, they are built on the foundation of human connections.

So, how can you foster these connections effectively?

## The Need for Human Connection

First, human connection is a fundamental and innate desire that is intricately woven into our very existence. It is an integral part of our identity as social beings, rooted in our evolutionary history as communal creatures. Recognizing and acknowledging this deep-seated need for connection is the first step toward effectively creating and nurturing meaningful relationships.

From the dawn of human civilization, we have thrived in communities, forming bonds, and relying on one another for survival, support, and companionship. Our capacity for empathy, compassion, and cooperation has been a driving force behind our collective progress. Understanding the significance of these social bonds can profoundly influence your approach to building connections in the context of social impact.

When you recognize that human connection is not merely a by-product of our interactions but a fundamental aspect of our existence, you begin to appreciate the inherent value of forging meaningful relationships. It is a reminder that beneath the layers of roles, responsibilities, and objectives, there are individuals seeking connection, understanding, and belonging.

In our work, missions and objectives often take center stage, and it can be easy to overlook the human element. However, by acknowledging the innate human need for connection, you can infuse your approach with empathy, authenticity, and genuine care. This recognition serves as a guiding principle, reminding you that every interaction, partnership, and collaboration is an opportunity to honor the profound importance of human connection.

It all starts with this fundamental realization—the undeniable truth that we are inherently driven to connect, share, and belong. It is the foundation on which you can build relationships that not only amplify your impact but also enrich the human experience, creating a world where compassion, understanding, and collaboration thrive.

## The People at the Core of Your Mission

Second, it's essential to direct your focus toward the people who are at the core of your mission, both within your organization and the individuals you aim to serve. This involves going beyond the surface and truly acknowledging their stories, their unique struggles, and their deep-seated aspirations.

When you humanize the mission, shifting the spotlight from abstract objectives to the individuals involved, you set the stage for a profound connection that surpasses statistics and goals. It's about recognizing that every person engaged with your mission carries a rich background with a wealth of experiences, dreams, and challenges.

Within your organization, consider the tireless efforts, the dedication, and the unwavering commitment of your team members. Acknowledge their personal journeys and the sacrifices they make to drive the mission forward. This recognition fosters a sense of camaraderie and solidarity, strengthening the bonds that hold your team together.

Similarly, when working with the individuals you aim to serve, take the time to listen to their stories, understand their needs, and respect their autonomy. By honoring their narratives, you create a space where empathy flourishes, and genuine connections are forged. This approach transcends the transactional nature of impact work and instead centers on the profound humanity that unites us all.

## The Importance of Reciprocity

Third, embrace the concept of reciprocity. It's crucial to approach every interaction with the understanding that it's not solely about what others can do for you or your organization; it's equally about what you can do for them.

When engaging with individuals, partners, or communities, do so with a genuine desire to provide value, support, and assistance. Seek ways to contribute positively to their objectives and well-being. This mindset shift from self-centric to other-centric fosters an environment of mutual respect and trust.

Reciprocity in connections involves understanding the needs, aspirations, and challenges of the people you engage with and offering your assistance or expertise when appropriate. It's about actively listening, empathizing, and being responsive to their concerns. When individuals recognize that their interests are valued, they are more likely to engage in a deeper and more meaningful connection.

Let's consider a workplace scenario as an example. You work on a team where one of your colleagues, Jorge, is facing a challenging project deadline. You actively listen to his concerns and challenges regarding the project, empathize with the pressure he's under, and help when appropriate.

In this case, you decide to assist Jorge by volunteering to take on some of his less critical tasks to help him meet the deadline. Your willingness to step in not only eases his workload but also shows that you value his well-being and professional success. As a result, Jorge recognizes your genuine support and willingness to help, leading to a stronger bond between you and a more collaborative and productive work environment. This example illustrates how reciprocity in connections can foster teamwork, trust, and meaningful relationships.

The concept of reciprocity elevates connections from transactional to transformative. It encourages collaboration, shared objectives, and a sense of shared responsibility. By prioritizing the well-being and goals of others, you not only strengthen your connections but also create a positive impact that extends far beyond your immediate network.

## The Maintaining of Connections

Additionally, keep in mind that connections are not static; they require ongoing effort and attention. Regular communication, engagement, and appreciation are essential for maintaining and strengthening connections over time. Human relationships thrive on the nourishment of genuine care and attention.

Maintaining and strengthening these connections over time demands an ongoing commitment to nurturing them. This involves various aspects, including regular communication, active engagement, and genuine appreciation.

Consistent and open communication is crucial for any connection. Whether it's with partners, supporters, or individuals within your organization, staying in touch is key. Share updates, progress reports, and relevant information. Keep the lines of communication open, inviting feedback and questions. By doing so, you demonstrate your commitment to transparency and collaboration.

Active engagement is another vital component of connection maintenance. Actively participate in discussions, attend events, and engage with the communities you're a part of. Show genuine interest in the well-being and concerns of those you're connected with. By actively engaging, you not only stay connected but also reinforce your dedication to the mission or cause you share.

Appreciation is arguably the easiest but most underrated tool for connection maintenance. People thrive on feeling valued and recognized. Take the time to express your gratitude and appreciation for the support, contributions, and efforts of your partners, supporters, and team members. Celebrate achievements, milestones, and shared successes together. Acknowledging the role each person plays in your collective journey strengthens the bonds that tie your network together.

Remember that the effort you put into connection maintenance is an investment in the sustainability and impact of your mission. It demonstrates your commitment to the well-being and shared goals of the individuals and organizations you connect with, fostering a sense of trust and loyalty that can lead to lasting, productive, and impactful relationships.

## The Places We Connect

Finally, create places, spaces, and opportunities for people to connect authentically. This principle aligns with our previous discussion about creating online and offline social moments.

Events, workshops, online forums, and collaborative initiatives all serve as platforms where individuals can come together, share their experiences, and contribute their unique perspectives. These spaces are more than mere gatherings; they are places where connection can take root and flourish.

When organizing events, consider the atmosphere and activities that encourage interaction. Foster an environment where participants feel comfortable sharing their thoughts and ideas. Incorporate team-building exercises, icebreakers, or open discussions that promote bonding and trust among attendees. Allow people to engage in meaningful conversations and forge connections based on shared values and interests.

## Being Authentic Means Being Vulnerable

When people have a high level of authenticity, they feel a true connection with others. This is because authentic people are willing to take risks in relationships without worrying about the outcome. They also don't see vulnerability as a weakness. Instead, they view it as a strength that makes them a great person to be around. If we want to connect with people, we need to be ready to be authentic as well. And to be authentic, we need to be ready to show parts of ourselves that are not necessarily the best or the prettiest; we need to be vulnerable and able to show this side to others as well as make sure that we are *truly* connecting with people, as opposed to only connecting with them on a rather shallow level.

People who are authentic are also willing to listen to others. They respect the boundaries of others and their preferences. Authenticity also means managing emotions. It's okay to express anger, sadness, disappointment, and frustration, but it's not okay to ignore or override other people's feelings—and this is part of being authentic. As authentic people, we are willing to accept that we are who we are, but we also know that we need to respect other people. Likewise, we allow ourselves to be vulnerable enough to express these emotions, as opposed to hiding them and acting as though we are always fine. The reason behind this is simple: the more authentic and vulnerable you show yourself to be, the more trustworthy you are, and, hence, the deeper the connections you can make.

There are also many different ways to show up as an authentic person. For example, sharing your stories can help you to develop deeper emotional connections with other people. This also adds depth to your why, because others look to you for opportunities to connect with shared experiences.

If you are worried about being vulnerable, start by making small changes in your personal life before you try doing so in a more professional sphere. You can begin by sharing your stories with a close friend or partner and get comfortable sharing these parts of yourself that are deeper as opposed to the typical superficial way we might speak to people we do not know. Otherwise, you can join a group online and practice this skill with them. In any case, being authentic requires you to start sharing your real, unfiltered self, and that is how we are able to connect deeply with people.

Being vulnerable can be scary, but it's necessary if you want to have a better connection with other people. Whether you share your story with your neighbors, coworkers, or partners, your honesty will make them feel like you care enough about the connection you have with them and about their time because you are willing to share true moments.

Very few people around me knew about my history with cancer or my relationship with Make-A-Wish. I grew up with scars that I hid, and I felt that those experiences didn't define who I was. However, as my work in social impact crystalized, I realized that it was these lived experiences that added depth to who I was, why my passion aligned with impact, and ultimately helped to foster early and deep connections within the communities I was joining. Your power is in your purpose, and your purpose can be found in your story. It takes time to find the clues, but as you allow yourself to become more vulnerable, your purpose begins to shine through.

## Nurture Your Connections

Social impact is not social without our connections. They form the bonds that unite individuals, organizations, and communities in a common mission to drive positive change. However, a connection, once established, is not a self-sustaining entity; it requires ongoing care and nurturing to thrive.

Don't forget or underestimate the importance of regular check-ins. Whether you're dealing with partners, collaborators, donors, volunteers, or team members, taking the time to check in on them is essential. Ask how they are doing, listen actively to their responses, and show genuine empathy. By doing so, you demonstrate that you value their presence and contributions, reinforcing the connection you share.

Maintaining connections involves the art of follow-up. When you meet someone at an event, a conference, or through your work, make an effort to follow up afterward. Send a thoughtful email, schedule a call, or even arrange a face-to-face meeting if possible. This follow-up demonstrates your commitment to fostering the connection beyond the initial meeting.

In your organization, don't overlook the importance of checking in with your staff members, team members, and other employees. Regularly engage in conversations about their experiences, concerns, and ideas. Encourage open communication and create a culture in which individuals feel comfortable sharing their thoughts. By addressing their needs and concerns, you strengthen the connections within your team and enhance their sense of belonging and commitment.

Connection maintenance extends online as well. Social media platforms provide opportunities for continuous engagement. Regularly interact with your online network, respond to comments and messages, and share valuable content. These actions keep the connection alive and demonstrate your commitment to staying connected.

# 8

# Championing Empathy

Empathy is an emotional connection that goes beyond rationality and data-driven decision-making. Although we might associate nonprofit and social impact work with statistics, strategies, and processes, empathy is the invisible thread that ties together meaningful connections, and ultimately, it's what drives success.

## The Power of Empathy

In impact work, the problems we aim to address are deeply rooted in human experiences. Poverty, inequality, health disparities, environmental challenges—these issues all have a profound impact on people's lives. To effectively address these problems, we must first understand and empathize with the individuals and communities affected by them. Empathy enables us to step into the shoes of others, to see the world from their perspective, and to truly comprehend their needs, struggles, and aspirations.

Empathy is the bridge that connects us to the people we serve, the partners we collaborate with, and the communities we aim to empower. It's the force that drives us to care deeply about the challenges others face and motivates us to take action to alleviate their suffering or improve their circumstances.

Consider, for instance, a nonprofit organization working to combat food insecurity. Through empathy, the organization's leaders and volunteers can genuinely understand the daily struggles of families who don't have access to nutritious meals. They can empathize with the parents who go to bed worried about their children's empty stomachs. This empathy fuels their determination to find innovative solutions, mobilize resources, and advocate for change that will make a real difference in these families' lives.

Empathy also plays a pivotal role in building strong and lasting connections. When we approach our interactions with empathy, we create an environment of trust, respect, and mutual understanding. We show others that we genuinely care about them and that we are committed to supporting their journey toward a better future.

Think about the power of empathy in the context of partnerships. When two organizations come together for a shared mission, it's not just about strategic alignment and shared objectives but also about the empathy that enables them to appreciate each other's strengths, challenges, and unique contributions. Empathy fosters a spirit of cooperation, collaboration, and shared responsibility.

In storytelling, empathy is the secret ingredient that makes narratives come alive. When we infuse our stories with empathy, we don't just convey facts and figures; we evoke emotions and create connections. A story told with empathy touches the hearts of its audience, inspiring compassion and a desire to act. It transforms data into human experiences, making complex issues tangible, relatable, and motivating people to get involved.

Consider a campaign to raise awareness about refugee rights. By sharing the personal stories of refugees with empathy, we enable the audience to feel the fear, hope, and resilience of these individuals. Empathetic storytelling breaks down barriers and builds bridges between diverse communities, fostering a sense of solidarity and support.

Empathy is not a fixed trait; it's a skill that can be cultivated and honed. To become more empathetic, we must be open to listening and learning from others. We should actively seek out diverse perspectives and engage in conversations that challenge our preconceived notions. Through active listening and reflection, we can broaden our understanding and deepen our capacity for empathy.

Empathy extends beyond our professional lives; it's a quality that enriches our personal relationships and contributes to our overall happiness. When we approach our friends, family, and loved ones with empathy, we strengthen our bonds and create a nurturing and supportive environment.

## Understanding Empathy

Let's first start by looking at what we mean with empathy in the context of an organization. Here, the term empathy refers to the ability to understand and share the feelings of others, even if we are not personally affected by their situation, or if we are not directly linked to it. It is the ability to put ourselves in someone else's shoes and to understand their perspective. In the context of social impact, empathy is crucial for communicating the needs and struggles of the people and communities we are supporting. To understand what this looks like in action, let's look at a few examples of scenarios.

## A Nonprofit Organization That Works with People Experiencing Homelessness

Imagine a nonprofit organization dedicated to people experiencing homelessness. Within this organization, the staff members and volunteers recognize the immense importance of empathy in their work. They don't merely see homelessness as a societal issue; they perceive it as a deeply human experience, riddled with complex emotions and individual stories.

In their approach, they take the time to sit down with people who are experiencing homelessness. They initiate conversations that go beyond the surface, aiming to understand the unique challenges, fears, and hopes that each individual carries. This deliberate effort to empathize with the person's specific circumstances enables them to provide highly personalized support.

Through these empathetic interactions, the organization's team members trade places with those they aim to help. They feel the weight of the struggles faced by each person, not just as an abstract concept but as a palpable reality. This empathy fuels their commitment to creating tailored solutions and support systems that address the nuanced needs of these individuals. It transforms empathy into actionable change.

Empathy serves as the link between recognizing a problem and driving meaningful transformation. It's not enough to comprehend the issue intellectually; you must also feel its impact on a deeply emotional level. Emotions are the driving force behind action, and empathy ignites the spark that propels change forward.

When an organization empathizes with the individuals it serves, their stories become more than narratives; they become windows into shared experiences. By conveying these stories with empathy, organizations can bridge the gap between abstract problems and tangible emotions.

For instance, consider a storytelling campaign designed to raise awareness about homelessness. Rather than relying solely on statistics and facts, the campaign centers on the personal stories of individuals who have experienced homelessness. These stories are infused with empathy, enabling the audience to connect not just with the data but with the human beings behind it.

When a person listens to the story of someone who has endured homelessness, told with empathy, they don't just absorb information; they experience empathy themselves. They empathize with the fear of not knowing where to sleep at night, the frustration of trying to secure a meal, and the hope for a better future. Empathetic storytelling doesn't just inform; it transforms passive listeners into active advocates for change.

Empathy converts social impact efforts from theory to practice. It's the driving force behind understanding, action, and transformation. By incorporating empathy into every facet of their work, organizations can ensure that their mission is not just a distant goal but a deeply felt commitment to making the world a better place—one empathetic connection at a time.

## A Company That Creates Consumer Products

Let's consider a different example—a company that specializes in producing consumer products, with a primary focus on sustainability. In their journey toward creating a positive social and environmental impact, they recognize the pivotal role empathy plays in their interactions and decision-making.

As they collaborate with an organization dedicated to listing and promoting companies that exclusively use sustainable products, a transformative process occurs. Rather than treating sustainability as a buzzword or a checkbox on their corporate agenda, the company's management team invests time and effort in comprehending the profound impact their products have on the environment and the communities affected by their operations.

Empathy becomes the basis of their approach. They stop looking at their products in isolation and begin to see the intricate web of relationships connecting their goods to the world around them. They empathize with the people whose lives are intertwined with their products, as well as the ecosystems that bear the brunt of their production processes.

This journey of empathy leads them to profound realizations. They start to feel the challenges faced by the communities affected by their operations—the hardships endured by local residents, the environmental degradation witnessed firsthand, and the aspirations for a better life that remain unfulfilled. This empathetic understanding transcends sympathy; it ignites a genuine desire to effect meaningful change.

Empowered by empathy, the company's management team initiates a comprehensive reassessment of their operations. They conduct a deep dive into their supply chains, scrutinizing every stage for opportunities to minimize negative environmental impacts. Their empathy extends to the very source of their materials, prompting them to seek sustainable alternatives and ethical sourcing practices.

They recognize that their products are not just commodities but instruments of change. Each purchase carries the potential to drive positive impact or perpetuate harm. This realization fuels their commitment to crafting products that align with their empathetic ethos. They prioritize sustainable materials, ethical production methods, and fair labor practices.

But their journey doesn't end there. Empathy motivates them to go beyond minimizing harm and actively seek ways to make a positive difference. They channel their resources into community engagement initiatives, supporting local development projects, and fostering partnerships with organizations dedicated to social and environmental causes.

Although the transformation is substantial and resource-intensive, it exemplifies the role that empathy plays in organizations committed to humanizing issues and nurturing meaningful relationships. In this scenario, empathy isn't a fleeting sentiment; it's a guiding force that empowers the company to evolve from a profit-driven entity to a compassionate and responsible steward of social and environmental care.

When empathy becomes an integral part of an organization's DNA, it transcends rhetoric and shapes every decision, every action, and every relationship. It fuels a commitment to making a positive impact—one created from genuine understanding and care, not from obligation.

## A Community Development Organization

As a final example of empathy, imagine a community development organization that works with low-income families in a specific area, perhaps even in your locale.

Members of this organization, which include dedicated volunteers and passionate staff members, invest substantial time immersing themselves within the community. They don't just sporadically visit the area or interact with residents in a superficial way; they become integral parts of the community, actively engaging and building genuine relationships.

This immersion is not without purpose. It serves as the foundation for building empathy. They walk the same streets of the residents, listening to their stories, struggles, and aspirations. By genuinely empathizing with the residents' daily experiences, the organization gains a deep understanding of their unique needs and challenges.

This understanding is the motivation behind their initiatives. They tailor their programs and services to directly address the specific needs they have uncovered. For instance, if they discover a significant portion of residents struggling to secure stable employment, they launch job training programs designed to equip individuals with the skills needed to access better job opportunities.

The organization doesn't stop at addressing immediate concerns. Their empathy extends to the next generation, where they identify children facing academic challenges due to their circumstances. In response, they develop educational programs aimed at narrowing the learning gap and providing these children with the support they need to thrive in school.

However, empathy doesn't limit itself to program development. It powers their advocacy efforts as well. The organization's deep understanding of the community's needs empowers them to be effective advocates for policy changes that will directly benefit residents. One such example is their unwavering commitment to advocating for a living wage, recognizing that economic stability is foundational for a better quality of life.

But the most impactful outcome of this empathetic approach is the profound human connections it nurtures. These connections go beyond the traditional roles of service provider and recipient, transforming into authentic bonds of trust, mutual respect, and shared aspirations.

Through their empathetic approach, the organization demonstrates that social impact is not only about providing solutions but also about forming meaningful and lasting connections with those they serve. Their commitment to empathy humanizes the process of social change, ensuring that every interaction, program, and initiative is infused with understanding and care.

In the end, this community development organization's journey is a testament to the immense power of empathy. It showcases how empathy, when integrated into the core of an organization's mission, has the potential to spark real and sustainable change.

## Becoming a More Empathetic Person

On a societal level, empathy is crucial for promoting social and emotional well-being. It can help promote kindness and understanding, leading to a more inclusive and compassionate society. Empathy can also play an important role in social impact and social change. As more empathetic people, we are better positioned to take actions that promote social justice and equality to create a better world for all. We are better able to put other people's needs forward and to care for them, making this world a better place for everyone.

Practicing empathy in your daily life isn't just about adding another to-do to your busy schedule; it's about adopting a fundamental approach to your interactions, underscored by authenticity and openness. Empathy is a powerful tool for building authentic connections and strengthening relationships, which in impact work becomes an integral part of your everyday life.

One of the key aspects of empathy in daily interactions is its authenticity. It's not about putting on an act or following a set of predetermined steps. Instead, it involves genuinely understanding and acknowledging the feelings and experiences of others. It's about embracing authenticity in your interactions, as I've discussed elsewhere in this book. Authentic empathy is about being present and truly listening, not just hearing the words but recognizing the emotions, concerns, and aspirations behind them.

When you practice empathy authentically, it becomes ingrained into who you are, shaping your responses and actions in various situations. You don't compartmentalize empathy into specific circumstances; it becomes a natural way of engaging with the people and world around you. Whether you're talking with friends, working on partnerships, or addressing concerns in your projects, authentic empathy guides your responses and fosters trust in your relationships.

Open-mindedness is another crucial component of empathy in everyday interactions. Being open to diverse perspectives and willing to adjust your own viewpoint is essential for cultivating empathy. Empathetic individuals acknowledge that people have different experiences, backgrounds, and beliefs, and they make a concerted effort to put themselves in others' shoes to better understand their thoughts and emotions. If you are able to openly listen to new information, use it in discernment in your current position, and then change your mind because of this new information and viewpoint, that is a superpower—one that should be celebrated and openly shared as a testament to the power of empathy and flexibility.

Empathetic listening is a practice that amplifies empathy in everyday interactions. It involves actively and attentively listening to a person's needs, emotions, and concerns. By listening with empathy, you gain insight into the other person's perspective and emotions, which can lead to more harmonious and productive relationships.

Empathetic listening is particularly valuable in collaborative settings, such as teamwork and partnerships. It enables you to step back, consider the circumstances influencing someone's thoughts or feelings, and approach the situation with a nonjudgmental attitude. This practice helps prevent hasty judgments and encourages thoughtful consideration of the other person's viewpoint.

Empathetic listening can also contribute to improved interpersonal conflict resolution. When you take the time to understand the emotions and motivations underlying a disagreement, it becomes easier to find common ground and work toward a mutually beneficial solution. Empathy enables you to recognize that reactions and behaviors may be influenced by external factors or personal challenges, fostering compassion and understanding in conflict resolution.

When you practice empathy, remain open-minded, and engage in empathetic listening, you'll find yourself developing not only a better awareness of others but also of yourself. As you navigate your journey toward becoming a more empathetic individual, remember that empathy is a continuous process of growth and self-reflection. It's about recognizing the multifaceted nature of human experiences, appreciating diversity in perspectives, and embracing the profound impact empathy can have on your interactions and relationships.

## Welcoming More Empathy in Your Office

Fostering empathy within your organization goes beyond just understanding the beneficiaries of your social impact efforts. It extends to all stakeholders involved in your mission, including partners, donors, volunteers, and employees. Each of these groups has their own unique perspectives, motivations, and expectations.

Within an organization, the team and its employees are the determinants of its success. They are the driving force behind the day-to-day operations, and their dedication and commitment are essential to achieving its mission. Nurturing empathy is not just an act of kindness but also a strategic approach to cultivating a motivated and high-performing team.

Just like the people an organization serves, its staff members also have their own unique perspectives, motivations, and challenges. By understanding and acknowledging their individual needs, you can create an environment that encourages their personal and professional growth.

When people feel heard and valued, they are more likely to be engaged, productive, and passionate about the organization's mission. Acknowledging and addressing their aspirations within can lead to higher job satisfaction and lower turnover rates.

Incorporating empathy into an organizational culture can also create a sense of inclusivity and belonging among the staff members. When employees perceive that their voices matter and that their needs are being met, it fosters a positive and collaborative atmosphere. In this environment, individuals are more inclined to work together, supporting one another and collectively striving for the organization's goals.

It's essential to understand that empathy for employees goes beyond surface-level actions. It requires a comprehensive approach that considers them holistically. This includes providing a supportive work-life balance, understanding their key motivations, recognizing and celebrating their achievements, and offering opportunities for professional development and growth. This will lead to a better and fully functional organization, which ultimately will lead to greater impact.

The significance of empathy within an organization can't be overstated. When employees feel heard, understood, and valued, they are more likely to be engaged, satisfied, and committed to their work. Empathy creates an environment where individuals are not just seen as cogs in a machine but as human beings with their own unique experiences and emotions.

An empathetic workplace culture fosters a sense of belonging and psychological safety. When employees know that their concerns and perspectives are genuinely considered, they are more likely to speak up, share ideas, and collaborate effectively. This open communication contributes to innovation, problem-solving, and overall organizational success.

Empathy plays a pivotal role in employee well-being and mental health. In today's fast-paced and often stressful work environments, having leaders and colleagues who show empathy can alleviate stress and prevent burnout. It creates a support system where individuals feel comfortable seeking help when needed.

Empathy also enhances leadership effectiveness. Leaders who understand and connect with their team members on a personal level can better motivate, inspire, and guide them toward achieving shared goals. Empathetic leaders create a positive work culture that attracts and retains top talent.

Empathy should be embedded in the organization's values and practices. Let's take a look at some key strategies to foster empathy among employees and create a more empathetic workplace.

## Lead by Example

Leading by example is a fundamental principle for fostering empathy within an organization. When the leadership team consistently demonstrates empathetic behavior in their interactions with employees, it sets a strong baseline and sends a powerful message to the entire team. Employees look to their leaders for guidance and inspiration, and when they witness empathetic leadership, it encourages them to embrace empathy in their own interactions. This creates a domino effect throughout the organization, where empathy becomes a shared value and a standard way of relating to one another. When leaders prioritize empathy, they not only enhance employee morale but also set the foundation for a more inclusive, collaborative, and compassionate workplace culture.

## Feedback Mechanisms

By creating accessible channels where employees can voice their concerns and share feedback, you signal that their opinions matter. It is also equally important to make sure that the collected feedback is also followed by action. When employees see that their feedback leads to tangible improvements or changes, it reinforces the idea that their voices are genuinely valued. This, in turn, fosters a culture of trust and openness, where employees feel safe to express themselves. Active listening and responsive actions strengthen the bond between employees and the organization, contributing to a more empathetic and engaged team.

## Recognition and Appreciation

Recognition and appreciation are powerful tools for fostering empathy within an organization. When leaders take the time to acknowledge employees' hard work and unique contributions, it sends a clear message that their efforts are seen and valued. Personalized recognition, tailored to an individual's specific accomplishments, not only boosts morale but also demonstrates a deep understanding of their role and impact. This recognition can be public or private, but it should always be sincere and genuine. When employees feel appreciated and understood, they are more likely to connect emotionally with the organization and its mission, resulting in a more empathetic and committed workforce.

## Flexible Work Arrangements

The way we work has undergone significant transformation, largely due to the pandemic. It has reshaped office and work culture, highlighting the importance of flexibility in our professional lives. Flexible work arrangements empower employees to better manage their work-life balance. Real people run real companies, and these real people have real lives outside of work. They might have doctor's appointments, sick children, soccer games, or dance recitals to attend. Recognizing the need for flexible arrangements acknowledges the humanity of your team members.

By allowing employees the autonomy and agency to accomplish their tasks while also honoring their daily lives, organizations create an atmosphere of trust and empathy. This approach fosters a sense of understanding among colleagues, recognizing that everyone's circumstances are unique. Whether it's remote work options, flexible hours, or compressed workweeks, offering flexibility demonstrates empathy and support for employees' personal lives. This, in turn, contributes to a happier and more engaged workforce, ultimately benefiting the organization's success.

## Professional Development

Professional development has often been overlooked in social impact, if not entirely forgotten. Just as empathy extends to understanding the personal lives of employees, it also encompasses their professional aspirations and growth.

To nurture empathy within your organization, take the time to understand each employee's career goals and ambitions. What are their passions, interests, and the skills they wish to acquire? By recognizing these individual trajectories, organizations can tailor development plans to align with their employees' desires and the company's mission. Investing in professional development not only enhances employees' skills and knowledge but also conveys that the organization values their growth and success.

## Empathy as a Core Value

Empathy should be thoughtfully and sincerely integrated into the mission and culture. By explicitly stating empathy as a core value in mission statements, employee handbooks, and company-wide communications, the organization sends a powerful message. It emphasizes that empathy isn't just a desirable trait but an integral part of the organization's identity.

This clarity fosters a culture where empathy is not only encouraged but expected. It guides interactions, decision-making, and overall behavior within the organization. By upholding empathy as a foundational principle, the organization solidifies its commitment to understanding and valuing the perspectives, needs, and well-being of its employees, stakeholders, and the communities it serves.

By prioritizing empathy in your organization, you not only create a more compassionate and supportive work environment but also empower your employees to better serve the mission and vision of the organization. Empathy is a two-way street, benefiting employees and the organization as a whole.

## Ask the Right Questions

The ability to ask the right questions is a key component in developing empathy in the workplace. This is especially true when it comes to fostering a culture of empathy within an organization. Asking the right question can help you uncover useful information and learn from the other person's perspective, which then allows you to understand and address the problem with empathy. In fact, we unfortunately often find ourselves assuming things about people when the simple act of asking a question would help us better understand the situation. Then, we also find ourselves assuming the worst, or thinking that a situation is what it is for reasons that we are mistaken about. This culture of assumption can lead to many misunderstandings in an organization, and, yet, it is easily avoided!

A deep dive question is a great way to uncover the why of the matter. For example, a simple question such as "What did you think?" can give you a good idea of how the other person feels, but it won't tell you what they actually want. However, asking "Why do you want this to happen this way" asks them exactly what they want, which opens up the floor for a deeper conversation and enables you to show empathy for any concerns they might have. Empathy can be difficult to cultivate if you don't have the proper communication skills. But, with a little effort, you can turn into a better listener and a more effective communicator. Likewise, with the right training, you can also bring your team up-to-date with this skill to ensure that everyone on your team is able to communicate with empathy—something that can truly boost your organization's impact in the long run.

## Create a Culture of Understanding and Appreciation

A culture of appreciation is a powerful way to boost employee morale. It has been shown to increase productivity, reduce absenteeism, and enhance staff loyalty, namely because it supports employees' efforts to feel heard, understood, and valued in your organization. Ultimately, they are the ones working on the projects you care about, so it's crucial that you know how to make them feel appreciated and understood!

Establishing a culture of appreciation within an organization is a multifaceted process that requires careful planning and consistent effort. It is not merely a matter of recognizing the importance of appreciation but also of putting practical steps into action to cultivate this culture effectively. Here are just a few positive yet powerful ways to do this:

- **Defining a clear mission and vision.** The foundation of an appreciation culture begins with a well-defined mission and vision for the organization. These guiding principles serve as a compass, directing the organization's efforts and goals. When the mission and vision are clear, employees have a better understanding of the organization's purpose and objectives. This clarity fosters a sense of togetherness because individuals align themselves with a common mission. It also provides a context within which appreciation can thrive.

- **Consistency and communication.** Once the mission and vision are established, consistency is key. The organization's leadership should consistently reinforce these guiding principles through clear and transparent communication. This communication should not be limited to occasional reminders but should permeate the organization's culture, becoming a part of its DNA. When leaders consistently communicate the mission and vision, employees are more likely to internalize these principles and integrate them into their daily work. As a result, appreciation becomes a natural part of the organization's culture, because individuals recognize the importance of acknowledging contributions that align with the mission.

- **Lead by example.** Effective leadership plays a pivotal role in shaping the culture of appreciation. Leaders must lead by example, demonstrating appreciation through their actions and interactions. When employees observe leaders genuinely valuing and appreciating the contributions of team members, it sets a precedent for the entire organization. This modeling of appreciative behavior encourages others to follow suit, creating a ripple effect throughout the workplace. Leadership that practices appreciation fosters an environment of trust and respect, making employees feel heard and valued.

- **Creating opportunities for appreciation.** Beyond leadership examples, organizations should create diverse opportunities for expressing appreciation. Although it may not always be possible to individually thank each employee for every contribution, there are numerous ways to collectively acknowledge and show appreciation. Simple acts of service, such as team recognition events or awards ceremonies, can serve as powerful gestures of gratitude. These occasions provide a platform to celebrate achievements, both big and small, and publicly acknowledge the efforts of employees. Establishing regular practices for recognizing outstanding work reinforces the culture of appreciation.

- **Supporting employees when they need it most.** Appreciation is not limited to scheduled events or awards; it should extend to moments when employees need support the most. Recognizing and addressing employees' challenges, whether personal or professional, is a fundamental aspect of an appreciation culture. Empathetic responses to difficulties, such as health issues or family emergencies, demonstrate that the organization values its employees as individuals, not just for their work contributions. This support during challenging times strengthens the bonds of trust and empathy within the organization.

Empathy is an invisible and essential force that powers successful organizations. It empowers us to genuinely connect with those struggling with challenges we're committed to addressing, enabling us to comprehend their experiences, needs, and hopes, ultimately shaping more effective and compassionate approaches and solutions.

# 9

# Using Social Moments, Partnerships, and Human Elements Collectively

Although individually potent, each of the elements in the SPH framework possesses its unique strengths and contributions to social impact. Social moments, with their ability to bring diverse individuals and organizations together, serve as a springboard for inspiration and innovation. These events are fertile grounds for the sharing of experiences, the formation of new ideas, and the initiation of collective actions. They can act as a spark that ignites empathy and understanding, fueling action while expanding the scope and depth of social impact initiatives.

Partnerships represent the collaborative synergy essential for substantial social change. By combining the strengths, resources, and perspectives of various groups, partnerships enable the tackling of complex problems with a collective spirit. When these partnerships embrace empathy as a guiding principle, they become not only more effective but also deeply compassionate. The core values of empathy and understanding influence decision-making processes, ensuring that progress, positive outcomes, and tangible impact are at the forefront of every collaborative effort.

Empathy, at the literal heart of this framework, serves as the driving force. It is the basis of compassionate and human-centered action. The cultivation of a culture of empathy within organizations and partnerships brings about a transformative shift in people's approach. It encourages active listening, compassionate decision-making, and a genuine understanding of the needs and emotions of their teammates, partners, donors, supporters, volunteers, and mission beneficiaries. When empathy is integrated into the foundation of these initiatives, they become more than just projects; they become channels for impactful, meaningful, and lasting change.

Yet, it is the combination of these elements that truly unleashes their potential as multipliers of social impact. Social moments provide the setting for shared inspiration and creativity, igniting the collective spirit of change. Partnerships offer the collaborative machinery to turn these inspirations into actions, mobilizing resources and expertise. Empathy, as the guiding principle, ensures that these actions are deeply rooted in understanding and compassion, thereby maximizing their effectiveness and ensuring long-term focus. Together, these elements serve as a comprehensive framework, leading to inspirational outcomes that are capable of addressing the most pressing challenges.

This holistic approach signifies the fusion of empathy, collaboration, and inspiration into a cohesive whole, enabling organizations, individuals, and communities to create a more compassionate and equitable world. By harnessing the unique strengths of each element, and coordinating them with a clear focus on shared values, social impact initiatives can achieve profound and lasting change.

# Leveraging Social Moments for Partnership Building

The strategic use of social moments as an opportunity for partnership building is an intricate interplay of art and science, one that demands a nuanced understanding of human connections and the dynamics of collaboration. In this process, the identification of common goals, the facilitation of connections, and the inspiration of collective action are the essential pieces of amplified social impact. As communities come together during these pivotal moments, a space emerges where collaborations take root, grow, and extend their reach, ultimately fostering a more significant and enduring influence and impact.

To understand the power of social moments and the part they play in inspiring meaningful partnerships, it is first important to understand how partnerships form during social moments. This dynamic fusion of elements not only unites like-minded individuals and organizations but also sparks the collective spirit that propels change. It is a testament to the power of community, the potential of shared purpose, and the promise of working together to create improved outcomes. So how can these seemingly ordinary moments become extraordinary opportunities for building partnerships that hold the key to unlocking a new level of social impact?

## Identifying Common Goals

Building successful partnerships during social moments hinges on the ability to identify common goals that extend beyond the broader mission or initiative. These shared objectives and passions lay the initial groundwork for high-impact collaborations. Consider, for example, a community gathering centered on the theme of environmental sustainability. This type of an event naturally draws individuals and organizations dedicated to preserving the environment. The collective commitment to this cause establishes a firm foundation, offering a launchpad for more purposeful and goal-specific partnership opportunities.

In this context, environmental sustainability serves as a common thread that connects a diverse array of attendees. Although they may vary in backgrounds, expertise, and resources, the shared passion for environmental conservation unites them with a common purpose. Two professors from different academic institutions might find common ground for collaboration in environmental education. Health care professionals from various hospitals might discover opportunities to exchange best practices on reducing operating room waste, further contributing to environmental sustainability. Similarly, a start-up founder and a manufacturing employee could engage in discussions about innovative approaches to enhancing the sustainability of specific operational processes.

These diverse partnerships within the overarching theme of environmental sustainability demonstrate how social moments provide a unique platform for identifying and pursuing shared goals. What might initially appear as casual conversations during these events can evolve into powerful collaborations driven by a collective commitment to making a positive impact on the environment.

Partnerships born out of common goals during social moments are often marked by a blend of expertise, experiences, and resources. This diversity strengthens the partnerships, offering a broader perspective on addressing complex issues. It brings together individuals with complementary skills and knowledge, allowing for more innovative problem-solving.

Additionally, the network of connections formed during these moments can expand the reach of partnerships, which benefits the broader community.

Ultimately, the identification of common goals during social moments acts as a magnetic force that draws like-minded individuals and organizations into alignment, guiding them toward purposeful partnerships. By capitalizing on the shared commitment to specific objectives within a broader mission, these partnerships become dynamic engines for generating positive social impact.

The concept of shared goals as the basis for partnership development during social moments underlines the significance of intention and clarity in fostering collaborations. When participants converge with a clear understanding of their common goals, the foundation for impactful partnerships is laid, and the potential for achieving remarkable outcomes is significantly increased. This is a testament to the remarkable synergy that emerges when individuals and organizations with aligned passions unite with the intent of making a difference in their shared area of value alignment.

## Facilitating Connections

An important consideration when planning social moments is creating spaces and opportunities where attendees can connect with potential collaborators. These spaces come in various forms, from structured networking sessions to interactive workshops, or even happy hours with some informal breakouts, all with the common goal of providing opportunities for meaningful interactions that lay the groundwork for future partnership initiatives.

Networking sessions serve as dynamic platforms where attendees can initiate conversations, exchange ideas, and explore the potential synergies between their respective organizations. These sessions are often organized to include elements such as brief introductions, pitch opportunities, or roundtable discussions, all of which are meticulously designed to facilitate organic connections.

The key to the effectiveness of networking sessions lies in their emphasis on relationship building over immediate dealmaking. Attendees have the opportunity to create connections based on understanding and shared values. By encouraging open and genuine conversations, these sessions enable attendees to explore common ground, identify mutual interests, and lay the foundation for future collaborations.

Interactive workshops provide a hands-on approach to partnership building, offering participants the opportunity to work together on collaborative projects or brainstorm innovative solutions to common challenges. These activities not only promote teamwork but also enable potential partners to assess each other's working styles, problem-solving approaches, and areas of expertise. In a relaxed and cooperative atmosphere, individuals and organizations can develop a deeper understanding of each other's capacities and potential contributions to shared goals.

Consider an interactive workshop at a social moment centered on education reform. Participants from diverse backgrounds, including educators, tech professionals, and policy advocates, come together to brainstorm solutions for enhancing digital learning in underserved communities. Throughout the workshop, participants share their insights, expertise, and innovative ideas, gaining valuable insights into each other's strengths and the potential for collaboration. As they collaborate on projects or work through complex challenges, they develop a sense of how they complement one another's skills and the possibilities for working together on broader educational initiatives.

Interactive workshops also facilitate relationship building in real time, because participants have the chance to understand the working dynamics of potential partners. This hands-on approach promotes mutual trust and respect, allowing for more informed and fruitful collaboration in the future.

Hackathons, with their condensed time frames and intense problem-solving atmosphere, have proven to be an effective model for innovation and collaboration. These events serve as platforms where diverse teams can quickly develop and showcase their solutions to complex problems. The concept of hackathons can be extended to social impact, offering a powerful means to harness collective creativity and drive change within communities.

Imagine a hackathon-style event dedicated to addressing pressing social issues, such as health care accessibility, environmental sustainability, or education reform. Teams of passionate individuals, each with unique skills and backgrounds, come together for a defined period, typically 24 to 48 hours. Their mission is to collaborate, innovate, and create solutions that address specific challenges within these domains.

The benefits of a hackathon model extend beyond the rapid development of solutions. The condensed time frame encourages participants to think creatively, work efficiently, and tap into a collective pool of knowledge and expertise. Additionally, the competitive aspect, with teams presenting their solutions to judges, fosters a culture of accountability and a drive for excellence. This setup can inspire participants to push their boundaries, think outside the box, and develop innovative strategies to tackle complex issues.

The solutions developed during these events can offer fresh perspectives, actionable plans, and prototypes that organizations, policymakers, and communities can adopt and implement. The collaboration and networking opportunities within these events may also lead to the formation of partnerships and ongoing initiatives dedicated to driving social progress.

These hackathons exemplify how the structure and energy of social moments can be strategically leveraged to maximize their impact. They provide an avenue for rapid problem-solving, foster innovation, and inspire collective action, making them a compelling tool for addressing pressing social challenges. By channeling the creativity and dedication of diverse participants, social impact hackathons become vehicles for meaningful change within communities and beyond.

## Shared Experiences and Learning

The significance of these spaces for partnership building is amplified by the shared experiences and learning that take place within them. Attendees not only connect with potential partners but also gain insights into the objectives, approaches, and capacities of different organizations. The exchange of knowledge and experience among participants is a valuable by-product of these spaces, fostering a culture of open communication and the sharing of best practices.

By offering environments conducive to meaningful interactions, these spaces contribute to the establishment of partnerships that are founded on a deep understanding of one another's missions, values, and operational capacities. This, in turn, paves the way for sustainable collaborations that have the potential to drive meaningful social impact.

The benefits of these spaces extend beyond the initial introductions. When attendees from diverse backgrounds and sectors come together during social moments, they often find themselves immersed in an environment rich with fresh perspectives and innovative ideas. Interactions at these events are characterized by a sense of shared purpose and a commitment to addressing social challenges collaboratively.

For example, at an environmental sustainability-focused social moment, a representative from an environmental nonprofit might find themselves in conversation with a sustainability expert from a tech company. This chance encounter sparks discussions on novel solutions, such as using data analytics to optimize resource conservation. Together, they may discover innovative approaches that neither party had considered on their own.

These spaces also provide a platform for those in attendance to witness the impact of diverse collaborations. Many social moments showcase the outcomes of partnerships formed during previous events, highlighting how collective action has led to tangible improvements. These success stories serve as inspiration and motivation for others to seek out similar partnerships and amplify their impact.

Ideally, the spaces created during social moments not only facilitate partnership building but also nurture a culture of collaboration and idea exchange. They offer an environment where individuals and organizations can learn from each other, embrace innovative approaches, and witness the transformative power of collective action. These experiences, combined with meaningful connections, lay the foundation for sustainable partnerships.

## Technology as a Facilitator

Technology plays a vital role in creating spaces for partnership building. Virtual meetings, seminars, webinars, conferences, and online collaboration platforms have become essential tools for connecting individuals and organizations, regardless of where they are physically located in the world. These digital spaces

# 152

IMPACT REDEFINED

facilitate not only networking and workshops but also serve as places for shared learning and knowledge exchange.

For example, an international social moment dedicated to empowering women in technology can leverage virtual spaces to bring together participants from around the world. Attendees can engage in real-time discussions, collaborative projects, and informative webinars. The digital platform allows for seamless connection and interaction, making it possible for like-minded individuals and organizations to build partnerships that extend beyond physical borders.

Creating spaces for partnership building in both physical and virtual spaces is a fundamental element of maximizing the potential of social moments. These spaces foster collaboration, encourage open communication, and facilitate knowledge sharing, ultimately contributing to the establishment of partnerships rooted in shared values and a profound understanding of each other's roles and contributions.

## Inspiring Collective Action

The power of social moments not only lies in connecting like-minded individuals and organizations but also in inspiring collective action. The impact of partnerships formed during these moments should be showcased to motivate others to join in and amplify the initiative's reach. This inspiration can take several forms, from the celebration of collaborative achievements to storytelling and visible results.

When communities witness the positive outcomes and transformative changes brought about by collaborative efforts, they become more inclined to participate and contribute. By highlighting the tangible results achieved through partnerships formed during these social moments, such as increased access to education or reduced environmental impact, individuals and organizations are encouraged to engage in similar ventures. It's a subtle way to create a fear of missing out when it comes to the next social moment you create.

Sharing real-life stories of how individuals, groups, or organizations have come together, overcome challenges, and made a difference can emotionally resonate with others. Through compelling narratives, people can envision their roles in similar partnerships and be inspired to take action.

Visible results are a testament to the potential of partnerships formed during social moments. When individuals can see the direct impact of these collaborations, it serves as a compelling call to action. For instance, witnessing a neighborhood revitalized through community partnerships or observing the reforestation of a previously barren area can ignite the desire to participate in initiatives that bring about positive change.

## Showcasing Success Stories

Broadcast, loudly and frequently, the achievements and success stories of collaborations that originated from previous social moments. Emphasize the specific, positive outcomes that were made possible through the collective effort of these partnerships. This is how you build motivation and inspiration. Leverage the success stories on social media to broaden the reach and awareness of these success stories in order to build a pipeline of interested and value-aligned support and participants.

## Encouraging Open Dialogue

Fostering an open dialogue within the community is an important step in inspiring collective action through partnerships. By creating a space where individuals can openly discuss the potential benefits of collaboration, you encourage participants to engage in meaningful conversations about their shared goals and aspirations. This dialogue serves as a basis for people to share their insights, challenges, and visions for collective projects, allowing for a free exchange of ideas and a deeper understanding of one another's perspectives.

Providing a supportive environment for communication stimulates interest and commitment to partnerships. This open dialogue not only facilitates the formation of partnerships but also nurtures a sense of belonging and shared purpose within the community, making it more likely for individuals to come together.

## Demonstrating Impact

Engaging participants in initiatives that have a clear and immediate impact is a compelling strategy to inspire collective action through partnerships. Activities such as community cleanups, tree-planting drives, or charity events offer participants the opportunity to experience the results of their collaborative efforts in real time. These hands-on experiences provide a direct connection between their actions and the positive change they can bring. When individuals see the immediate impact of working together, it serves as a powerful example for inspiring partnerships. They witness the significance of their collective contributions and are motivated to continue collaborating to address more complex social challenges and achieve even greater outcomes.

Ultimately, the art of leveraging social moments for partnership building lies in crafting an environment where individuals and organizations feel compelled to connect and collaborate on a shared journey toward a common goal. Through the identification of common objectives, the facilitation of meaningful connections, and the inspiration of collective action, social moments can transform into pivotal stepping stones in the pursuit of amplified social impact. These partnerships, driven by a commitment to realize change, have the potential to create lasting, transformative effects in our communities and beyond.

# Developing Empathy-Focused Partnerships

The strategic infusion of empathy into partnerships can be a powerful ingredient toward more meaningful, sustainable, and compassionate social impact. These partnerships prioritize the emotional state and experiences of the beneficiaries and foster a collaborative environment grounded in understanding and human connection. There are various strategies and practices that can help nurture empathy-focused partnerships that magnify the positive outcomes of programs and initiatives.

## Values Alignment

The foundational pillar of empathy-focused partnerships is the alignment of values. It is essential to prioritize partners whose values resonate with empathy and a human-centric approach when seeking collaborative opportunities, whether they are organizations or individuals.

The significance of values alignment lies in the shared commitment to prioritizing the feelings and experiences of the people and partners. When partners genuinely care about the people who carry out these initiatives, as well as the people they aim to serve, the partnership gains a solid foundation built on empathy.

This values alignment ensures that the core principles of compassion and understanding are at the forefront of the partnership's objectives. The shared commitment to empathy serves as their North Star, guiding the path toward creating initiatives that not only bring about positive social impact but also prioritize the needs and experiences of the individuals and communities involved.

Values alignment in empathy-focused partnerships goes beyond just organizational or personal compatibility. It is the harmonious blend of shared values that enables partnerships to extend their reach and influence in ways that touch the lives of those they intend to serve deeply.

## Empathetic Agreements

Embedding empathy within the core of partnerships can be achieved by incorporating empathy-focused clauses, commitments, or agreements into the partnership. This strategic step ensures that empathy remains not just a concept but an actionable and integral part of the partnership's DNA, setting clear expectations for how empathy will be used to sustain the partnership. The inclusion of empathetic agreements is like making a pledge to uphold empathy in all aspects of the partnership.

These agreements can serve as either a written or verbal declaration of the partners' shared intent to prioritize empathy. By codifying this commitment, partners reinforce their dedication to an empathetic approach, even as the partnership evolves.

These agreements and commitments could encompass a wide range of essential aspects. One critical facet involves ensuring that partnership members use beneficiary-centered language in all project-related communications and materials. This commitment is designed to guarantee that the voices of the individuals the initiative serves are not only acknowledged but also respected throughout the partnership.

Another crucial element is the promotion of inclusivity within the initiatives. Partners can formally agree to actively seek participation and feedback. This commitment fosters an environment of openness and empathy, offering a channel for their contributions and involvement.

The agreements may also place significant emphasis on the role of empathy in the decision-making processes of the partnership. This may involve actively considering different and new perspectives when shaping project strategies or evaluating the impact of these strategies.

Partners can make a commitment to cultivate a culture of continuous learning and improvement. This involves regular assessments of the empathy-driven approaches with the goal of making necessary adjustments and refinements as needed.

By incorporating these commitments, partners actively infuse empathy into their working relationships. They transform empathy from an aspirational concept into a tangible commitment, ensuring that, as the partnership progresses, empathy remains at its core.

### Challenges in Nurturing Empathy-Focused Partnerships

Empathy-focused partnerships hold immense promise for driving social impact; however, there are several common road blocks faced in cultivating these partnerships:

- **Lack of awareness.** One significant challenge arises from organizations' limited awareness or understanding of what it truly means to build an empathy-focused partnership. Though there has been concerted effort in business culture to nurture empathy, many partners might not possess a clear comprehension of how to integrate empathy into their collaborative efforts. Because of this, there is a compelling need for educational initiatives and accessible resources that can guide organizations in embedding empathy into their partnerships. Workshops, webinars, and mentorship programs have the potential to be instrumental in closing the knowledge gap.

- **Resistance to change.** Legacy think is pervasive in the impact space. The transition toward an empathy-focused approach can provoke resistance, particularly within organizations that have operated the same way for a long time, without any major organizational and philosophical adjustments. When this is the case, it's important to substantiate the merits of empathy-focused partnerships. This can be achieved through the presentation of case studies and success stories that illustrate specific and measurable benefits. Demonstrating the positive outcomes that these partnerships can generate is an effective way to alleviate resistance and encourage a shift in mindset.

- **Resource constraints.** Certain organizations may find themselves constrained in their ability to allocate adequate financial or human resources for nurturing empathy-focused partnerships. Collaboration with like-minded and synergistic organizations can offer opportunities for pooling resources and collective action.

- **Scaling challenges.** It can be a complex task to expand partnerships while upholding their empathetic nature. In response, organizations should explore the integration of technology solutions that are built for the specific use case or purpose of the partnership.

# Empathy as the Inspiration for Social Moments

Empathy has the power to infuse social moments with purpose, resonance, and inclusivity. By harnessing the power of empathy within these social moments, we can unlock their full potential as vehicles for positive social impact.

## Storytelling: Crafting Emotional Connections

One of the most powerful ways to embed empathy into social moments is through storytelling. Encouraging individuals to share their personal narratives can create profound empathy in online and offline social moments. Personal stories have a unique ability to humanize experiences and challenges, making them relatable to a broader audience. When someone shares their true and authentic journey, the ups and downs they've faced, and the lessons learned along the way, it evokes empathy by enabling others to emotionally connect with their story.

These narratives go beyond statistics and data, reaching the hearts of their audience. People can see a piece of themselves in the storyteller's journey, sparking empathy and understanding. This emotional connection often inspires action, whether it's a commitment to a cause, a decision to connect with a fellow supporter, or a realization that we're all part of a shared human experience.

Storytelling within offline social moments can be a structured part of the agenda, with designated individuals sharing their narratives. Alternatively, it can be a spontaneous and informal aspect, with attendees invited to open up about their own experiences. Creating a safe and nonjudgmental space is crucial, enabling people to share their stories authentically.

## Welcoming Diverse Perspectives

Empathy thrives in environments that value diversity and prioritize the voices of marginalized or underrepresented groups. To ensure that social moments are inclusive and resonate with a wide range of people, it is crucial to prioritize inclusivity in the planning and execution of these online and offline social moments.

## Diverse Representation

Whether online or offline, ensure that speakers, panelists, and storytellers represent a range of backgrounds, experiences, and perspectives. Diverse representation not only fosters empathy but also sends a powerful message of inclusivity to attendees. It ensures that audiences encounter a broad spectrum of back-grounds, experiences, and perspectives, which is pivotal for fostering empathy.

When social moments feature a diverse array of stories and storytellers, attendees are exposed to a wider range of experiences. This exposure can expand their horizons, challenge their preconceptions, and stimulate empathy by helping them under-stand the nuances of different lived experiences.

For offline events, a diverse lineup of participants mirrors the complexity of our society. It acknowledges that communities are multifaceted, and this recognition can resonate strongly with attendees. Seeing people from various backgrounds sharing their stories validates the experiences of those in the audience and reinforces the notion that everyone's story is worth telling.

Audiences of social moments are more likely to engage and empathize with individuals who share their or similar experiences. Diverse representation provides multiple entry points for engagement, ensuring that everyone can find someone whose story resonates with them. This diversity encourages active participation and fosters connections among people who may not have crossed paths otherwise.

## Listening and Open Dialogue

Create spaces within social moments for open dialogue and active listening. In online and offline settings, these practices can enhance engagement and cultivate a sense of inclusivity and shared understanding.

Online, social moments often take place through webinars, live streams, or online discussions. In these contexts, open dialogue can be facilitated through interactive Q&A sessions, real-time chats, and social media comments. Moderating these platforms to ensure that negative or harmful comments are addressed promptly helps maintain a safe and constructive space for audiences.

Encouraging audiences to share their perspectives, stories, and experiences during social moments is essential. By inviting participation, social moments can become a platform for individuals to express themselves, be heard, and contribute to the collective conversation. It's crucial that these shared voices are not only acknowledged but also considered when shaping the content and themes of future content.

Incorporating empathy into social moments involves intentionality and a commitment to fostering an environment where audiences feel valued and understood. These moments have the potential to serve as transformative spaces where empathy not only connects individuals but also inspires them to take meaningful action in the pursuit of positive social impact.

# Hypothetical Scenarios

We've explored a lot of important concepts in this chapter and in this book. We've examined the core social moments, partnerships, and human elements. This has included a lot of considerations such as storytelling, empathy, engagement, collaboration, outreach, social media, and more. How can we collectively integrate all of these ideas? Let's look at a few scenarios that illustrate how this can be done.

### Scenario 1: The Global Clean Water Initiative

Millions of people around the world face a harsh reality—lack of access to clean and safe drinking water. This dire situation not only affects their health but also perpetuates economic challenges and contributes to environmental degradation. To combat this global crisis, organizations have been harnessing the combined power of social moments, partnerships, and empathy, leading to remarkable social impact.

**The Challenge**   Access to clean and safe drinking water is a fundamental human right, yet it remains a pressing issue in many parts of the world, even in the United States. The consequences of water scarcity are far-reaching, affecting not only health but also livelihoods and the environment. Lack of access to clean water leads to waterborne diseases, which, in turn, result in high mortality rates, particularly among children. The time-consuming task of fetching water from distant sources, often done by women and children, takes time away from education and economic opportunities. The environment suffers as well because unsustainable practices lead to resource depletion and contamination of water sources.

**Social Moments**   The Global Clean Water Initiative's annual festival stands as the pillar of its social moments strategy. It is an event that captures attention offline and online, generating thousands of social media posts and reaching millions of people with tens of millions of impressions. This dynamic interplay between real-life engagement and online visibility significantly contributes to the initiative's success.

**Real-Life Engagement**   The festival is designed to be an immersive experience that fosters genuine connections among attendees. People from diverse backgrounds, cultures, and professions converge to partake in the event. They engage in discussions, share stories, and participate in activities aimed at raising awareness about water scarcity. This real-world engagement is vital in bringing people face-to-face with the issue and fostering empathy. Personal interactions, storytelling sessions, and empathy-building experiences provide a deeper understanding of the challenges faced by communities without access to clean water. Attendees leave the festival not only with a greater awareness of the issue but also with a sense of emotional connection to the cause.

**Online Visibility**   Through social media, the festival's impact extends far beyond its physical geography. Attendees, impassioned by their experiences, take to social media platforms to share their thoughts, stories, and images. The use of event-specific hashtags and tagging of the Global Clean Water Initiative's social media profiles generates a significant amount of buzz and social virality. These posts not only capture the essence of the festival but also reach a global audience. The power of social media amplifies the festival's reach, making it a trending topic online.

**Impressions and Outreach**   The collective effect of these social media posts results in an impressive number of impressions. Tens of millions of people share their authentic feelings, thoughts, and proclamations of action related to the festival, whether it's in the form of heartfelt stories, powerful images, or informative videos. This widespread outreach significantly contributes to raising awareness about water scarcity. It also inspires individuals who couldn't attend the event to take action, whether through donations, volunteering, or initiating their own awareness campaigns.

The Global Clean Water Initiative's festival success as a social moment is not confined to the festival days alone. Its impact reverberates through digitally, creating a wave of empathy, awareness, and support for the initiative's cause. This synergy between real-life engagement and online visibility underscores the profound influence that social moments can have when they are designed to be inclusive, impactful, and resonate deeply with their target audiences.

**Partnerships**   The initiative recognized that addressing water scarcity requires collaboration at multiple levels. Therefore, the organization sought partnerships with corporate sponsors, subject matter experts, and influencers. These partnerships were vital in securing funding for clean water solutions, ensuring the sustainability of projects, and scaling up their efforts. By working together, a united front was created to tackle water scarcity comprehensively.

**Corporate Partners**   A unique aspect of the Global Clean Water Initiative's festival is its ability to communicate tangible and mutual benefits to corporate partners. These partners are not only seen as benefactors but as integral components of the initiative. The organization offers its corporate partners a chance to align their brand with a socially responsible cause, enhancing their public image. By participating in the festival and supporting clean water projects, these corporations demonstrate their commitment to corporate social responsibility. This not only garners positive attention but also helps build customer loyalty. The organization provides corporate partners with comprehensive reporting and metrics that highlight the impact of their support. These metrics not only include mission-specific metrics, such as the number of communities served and the volume of clean water provided, but also important marketing metrics, such as reach, awareness, engagement, and brand sentiment. This approach reassures corporate partners that their contributions lead to concrete results and positive corporate brand outcomes.

**Influencer Partnerships**   In addition to corporate partnerships, the initiative has skillfully leveraged influencer partnerships. By collaborating with social media influencers, the initiative further amplifies its impact and reach. Influencers often participate in the festival, sharing their experiences and insights through their social media channels. Their endorsement and engagement bring the cause to the attention of a broader and more diverse audience. The integration of influencer partnerships significantly contributes to increasing awareness and garnering support. The shared empathy and personal engagement of these influencers with the festival's cause foster deeper connections with their followers. This deeper connection often translates into active engagement, including donations and volunteering. The influencer partnerships serve as a powerful means to expand the reach of the Global Clean Water Initiative, inspiring more individuals to join the cause and make a difference.

**Empathy**   Empathy is at the core of the initiative. Personal stories of individuals and communities affected by water scarcity are shared prior to the festival on social media as well as during the festival. These stories bring to life the daily struggles of those without access to clean water. Empathy-building experiences are a key component of the initiative, designed to help festival audiences better understand the challenges and hardships faced by these communities. By fostering empathy, the initiative aims to connect people on a deeply human level, transcending cultural and geographical boundaries.

**Elevating Human Interest Storytelling**   The Global Clean Water Initiative places a significant emphasis on human interest storytelling. It recognizes that empathy is often ignited when individuals can relate to the experiences, challenges, and triumphs of others. Knowing this, the festival incorporates storytelling into its core approach. Personal narratives of those affected by water scarcity are shared during the festival, and online before, during, and after. These stories highlight the daily struggles and resilience of communities without access to clean water. Through the power of storytelling, attendees can emotionally connect with these individuals, fostering a sense of empathy.

**Showcasing the Stories of Changemakers**  In addition to sharing the stories of those affected by the water crisis, the initiative also focuses on the stories of changemakers from the organization working tirelessly to address this global issue. Understanding the motivations and journeys of people who are committed to solving the clean water crisis provides insight into the driving force behind their empathy. By showcasing the stories of dedicated individuals, the initiative not only honors their efforts but also offers a glimpse into the passionate community working toward change. This approach highlights the human aspect of social impact and encourages others to get involved.

The combination of human interest storytelling and the showcasing of changemakers and supported communities not only deepens empathy but also inspires action. Attendees of the Global Clean Water Initiative's festival leave not only with a heightened awareness of the water crisis but also with a personal connection to the cause and the people involved in solving it. This personal connection often leads to active engagement, whether through financial contributions, volunteer work, or ongoing support. The human-centric approach taken by the initiative exemplifies how empathy, when integrated into social moments, can create a powerful and enduring impact.

The Global Clean Water Initiative serves as a compelling use case, demonstrating how a coordinated approach that incorporates social moments, partnerships, and empathy can bring about real change. The initiative not only addresses the pressing issue of water scarcity but also highlights the power of empathy to foster collaboration, inspire action, and make a substantial difference in the lives of people in communities around the world.

## Scenario 2: The Education Equality Movement

Inequities in access to quality education represent a pressing global challenge that affects individuals across diverse socioeconomic backgrounds and geographic locations. These disparities in educational opportunities not only challenge personal growth and development but also perpetuate cycles of poverty and social inequality. There is transformative potential of strategic initiatives, collaborative partnerships, and empathetic actions that can work together to address this critical issue and pave the way for a more equitable and promising future.

**The Challenge**    Disparities in access to quality education persist worldwide, hindering social and economic progress. Millions of children face barriers to receiving an education that empowers them to build a better future. This challenge demands innovative solutions and collaborative efforts.

**Social Moments**    A global education nonprofit recognized the importance of uniting stakeholders to address this issue; hence, the International Education Equality Day was born. Each year, this day serves as a platform for a diverse array of stakeholders, including educators, students, policymakers, and parents, to come together and collectively advocate for education equality. The event is not just a day of recognition but a catalyst for change, a social moment that compels everyone to become part of the solution.

At the heart of the International Education Equality Day is the intention to draw attention not only from those physically present but also from a global community through real-life and online channels. The event is strategically designed to maximize its reach and impact, taking advantage of technology and social media to amplify its message.

**Real-Life Engagement**   The event garners hundreds of attendees, including educators, students, policymakers, parents, and community members. The physical presence of these stakeholders creates an atmosphere of solidarity and urgency. It is a day when passionate individuals gather to voice their support for education equality. Their active participation, live interactions, and shared commitment to the cause resonate profoundly.

**Online Engagement**   The International Education Equality Day leverages social media platforms, live streaming, and digital campaigns to further expand its impact. This online presence transforms the event from a localized gathering into a global movement, as well as creates an additional forum for conversation and community building.

**Live Streaming**   Live streaming the event ensures that a global community actively participates, engages, and supports the cause. By broadcasting the event in real time, the event transcends geographical boundaries. Those who are unable to attend physically can still connect with the event virtually, making it an inclusive experience for a worldwide audience. The live stream enables individuals from different corners of the globe to witness the impactful stories and participate in important conversations, fostering a sense of belonging to a global community united by a shared commitment to education equality.

**Social Media Amplification**    The event's organizers encourage attendees to actively share their experiences and insights on social media platforms using dedicated event hashtags. These platforms serve as virtual spaces where individuals can express their support and share what they've learned. The power of social media lies in its ability to spark conversations, disseminate information, and inspire action. Social media posts related to the event generate discussions, raise awareness, and encourage individuals to get involved. The digital footprint left by these posts, retweets, shares, and comments creates an opportunity to reach people who may not have initially been aware of the event.

**Partnerships**    One of the key strengths of the International Education Equality Day lies in its ability to bring influential individuals and organizations together in the same room. By fostering an environment where educators, policymakers, students, parents, and experts from diverse fields converge, the event becomes a hotbed of innovative opportunities and ideas. The presence of influential figures sparks dialogue and ideation, enabling the creation of innovative strategies to address education disparities. These collaborations go beyond the event and extend into concrete action, ensuring that ideas translate into practical solutions for the education sector.

**Diverse Contributions**    The event is founded on a principle of inclusivity, inviting participation from a wide variety of stakeholders. This inclusive approach creates an opportunity for contributions that bring a wealth of innovative ideas and concepts.

Educators share insights derived from their firsthand experiences in classrooms, offering practical and contextually relevant solutions. Parents, possessing a deep understanding of the challenges faced by students, contribute valuable perspectives.

Policymakers offer insights into systemic changes that can lead to lasting improvements. And importantly, students themselves are recognized as contributors, providing insights into their unique educational experiences and needs.

This diverse set of perspectives and voices, collectively engaging in open dialogue and collaboration, fuels innovation and comprehensive problem-solving. It is this inclusivity and diversity that drive the success of the initiative, helping to formulate impactful policies and strategies that aim to address educational disparities effectively.

**Cross-Sector Collaboration** The International Education Equality Day goes beyond the traditional boundaries of the education sector, breaking down silos and facilitating cross-sector collaboration. This open approach welcomes professionals from diverse fields, including technology, health care, business, and more. These individuals bring with them a wealth of knowledge, fresh perspectives, and innovative tools that can significantly affect the quality of education.

By engaging professionals from different backgrounds, the event taps into a broader pool of expertise. For example, technology experts may introduce innovative learning platforms, health care specialists can provide insights into the intersection of health and education, and business professionals might contribute strategies for efficient resource allocation and management. These cross-sector collaborations harness the strengths and insights from each field to create a comprehensive approach to addressing education disparities.

Currently boundaries between disciplines are becoming increasingly fluid; solutions often emerge at the intersections of different fields. Cross-sector collaboration is the driving force behind addressing complex social issues such as education inequality. It allows for the blending of knowledge, expertise, and creativity from multiple sectors, resulting in holistic and effective solutions to benefit students, teachers, parents, and communities.

**Generating New Ideas**   The International Education Equality Day's focus on empathy-infused partnerships goes a step beyond conventional collaboration. This emphasis on empathy invites participants to view educational challenges through the lens of those most directly affected by disparities, creating a deeper understanding of their experiences and needs. This unique perspective serves as a driver of innovative, human-centered ideas capable of revolutionizing traditional education models. These ideas encompass a broad spectrum, from the introduction of new teaching methods that cater to individual learning styles to the integration of cutting-edge technology that enhances the educational experience. The event's empathetic approach supports the generation of fresh approaches and solutions to legacy problems in education, ultimately aiming to bridge gaps, remove barriers, and pave the way for a more equitable and inclusive education system.

**Empathy**   The strength of the International Education Equality Day lies in its ability to bring all perspectives to the table. To address the complex issue of education disparities, it recognizes the importance of considering input from all stakeholders. This includes students, teachers, parents, administrators, and public policymakers. The multifaceted nature of this work is founded on the understanding that the education system is a network of interconnected parts, and every perspective is vital to comprehensively address the challenges.

**Consensus, Compromise, Compassion**   Education equality is a multifaceted challenge, and addressing it requires more than just acknowledging multiple perspectives. It demands the ability to build consensus when possible, compromise when needed, and maintain compassion as an anchor throughout. The event recognizes that achieving real change often requires stakeholders to find common ground and work together toward shared objectives. In some cases, it may involve making compromises to accommodate various viewpoints and move forward effectively. Compassion is at the heart of these efforts. It reminds all involved that the ultimate goal is to create a more equitable and compassionate education system that benefits every student, teacher, and parent.

**Awakening a Collective Sense of Responsibility**   Empathy is not just an abstract concept in this initiative; it is a call to action. By sharing real-life stories, fostering understanding through shared experiences, and creating an environment of inclusivity, the event aims to awaken a collective sense of responsibility among all participants. This sense of responsibility transcends individual interests and becomes a shared commitment to addressing education disparities. In doing so, the initiative acknowledges the interconnectedness of all involved and recognizes that a systemic challenge necessitates a collective response.

**Cultivating Empathy as the Catalyst for Change**   Empathy is not just a value within this movement; it's what's driving change. The event acknowledges that empathy holds the power to deliver real progress in education. It cultivates empathy by encouraging individuals to look beyond their own experiences and truly understand the challenges and aspirations of others. By doing so, the initiative builds a stronger foundation for addressing education disparities collectively.

## Scenario 3: The Mental Health Awareness Revolution

Addressing ever-pressing global challenges necessitates innovative and multifaceted approaches. It requires a dynamic blend of elements that can galvanize individuals, organizations, and entire communities toward a common goal. The convergence of social moments, partnerships, and empathy can form an effective framework capable of activating transformative social impact. This initiative exemplifies how the integration of social moments, partnerships, and empathy is instrumental in combatting one of the most pervasive global issues of our time: mental health.

**The Challenge** Mental health issues transcend borders, affecting individuals across age groups, backgrounds, and walks of life. Stigma and inadequate access to mental health services perpetuate these challenges, making it essential to address mental health comprehensively. Never before has the need to grapple with the vast spectrum of mental health challenges been more apparent.

**Social Moments** The Mental Health Awareness Revolution differentiates itself from the traditional model of single-day events by embracing a more continuous approach. Instead, it offers a series of interconnected social moments that take place throughout the year. These social moments are designed to keep mental health issues consistently visible and relevant to the public. They take various forms, catering to different preferences and modes of engagement.

Some of these moments include large-scale community gatherings, providing a physical space for people to come together, share their experiences, and advocate for mental health support.

Additionally, the movement leverages online platforms, conducting webinars, virtual campaigns, and interactive initiatives that engage a global audience. This multifaceted approach ensures that the conversation about mental health remains dynamic, persistent, and inclusive. People from various backgrounds, age groups, and locations can engage with the movement in ways that are most accessible and meaningful to them. This continuous engagement helps keep mental health in the public consciousness and fosters ongoing support for those facing challenges.

**Partnerships** The Mental Health Awareness Revolution actively seeks to build partnerships with a diverse array of stakeholders. These partners encompass a wide range of entities, including mental health organizations, health care providers, universities, government agencies, community groups, and corporations. The diversity of partnerships reflects the holistic approach taken by the movement to tackle mental health challenges from multiple angles.

Mental health organizations are natural allies in this initiative because their expertise and experience contribute to the movement's credibility and impact. Health care providers play a crucial role by ensuring that individuals have access to the professional support they need. Universities and educational institutions collaborate to create environments that prioritize the mental well-being of students. Government agencies work with the movement to develop policies that enhance mental health services and accessibility, creating a supportive regulatory environment. Community groups serve as vital resources for individuals seeking local support and connection. Corporations, too, are essential partners because they can promote mental health awareness and support in the workplace.

These partnerships are instrumental in ensuring a comprehensive and inclusive approach to addressing mental health challenges. They contribute to policy changes, increase accessibility to mental health services, and offer a spectrum of community-based support. Such multidimensional collaboration fosters a more empathetic and effective response to mental health issues.

**Reduced Stigma and Increased Support**    One of the most significant accomplishments of the Mental Health Awareness Revolution has been its contribution to reducing the stigma about mental health, resulting in more individuals being willing to openly discuss their experiences. By sharing their mental health journeys without the fear of judgment or discrimination, more people are seeking help and support, which is an essential step toward better mental health for all. This increased openness has been critical in fostering understanding and empathy among individuals, communities, and society as a whole. By breaking down the barriers of stigma, the movement has created an environment in which mental health is openly acknowledged and discussed.

The network of empathetic partners established by the Mental Health Awareness Revolution plays a pivotal role in reducing stigma. These partners are not only allies in the cause but also valuable sources of support for individuals facing mental health challenges. The availability of support from a wide range of empathetic partners, which includes mental health organizations, health care providers, community groups, and more, ensures that assistance is readily accessible to those in need.

**Improved Policies and Services**    Collaborative efforts within the Mental Health Awareness Revolution have led to significant policy changes aimed at prioritizing mental health services and overall well-being. As a result, mental health services have seen increased funding, enabling them to be more accessible and comprehensive.

These policy changes extend beyond the health care sector, reaching into education systems as well. With a more empathetic approach, educational institutions are now better equipped to address the mental health and well-being of students. Schools and universities have begun incorporating mental health programs, counseling services, and well-being initiatives that cater to the emotional and psychological needs of students.

The improved policies and services, backed by a more empathetic approach, have ushered in an era of mental health awareness and care that is accessible and sensitive to the needs of individuals. These changes have created an environment in which mental health is not merely an afterthought but a significant and integral component of overall well-being.

**Empowered Communities**  The Mental Health Awareness Revolution has empowered communities at the grassroots level, encouraging them to take an active role in providing mental health support. The series of social moments organized by the movement have inspired local initiatives and support groups to form and thrive. These community-based efforts leverage the movement's resources and the empathy-driven partnerships, ensuring that they are connected to a broader network of support, information, and resources.

This local mobilization represents the tangible translation of the global movement into actionable, community-specific changes. The Mental Health Awareness Revolution's activities and events empower community members to become advocates, support providers, and provide resources for their peers and neighbors. It fosters an environment in which individuals take charge of their mental health and are well-equipped to support others facing mental health challenges. The result is a network of interconnected communities actively engaged in promoting mental health and emotional well-being, thereby strengthening the impact of the overall movement.

**Continuing the Momentum**   Sustaining the momentum generated by the Mental Health Awareness Revolution throughout the year and beyond is a formidable undertaking. It demands meticulous planning to keep the movement active and relevant. The effort goes beyond a singular event; it requires a continuous calendar of engaging events, campaigns, and activities that keep the subject of mental health at the forefront of public awareness. This includes leveraging various platforms, from physical community gatherings to online seminars and virtual campaigns. Maintaining community engagement and ensuring that mental health resources are consistently available for those in need is essential to keep the momentum alive.

**Balanced and Equitable Distribution**   Given the diversity of partners involved in the Mental Health Awareness Revolution, resource allocation can be complex. Ensuring a balanced and equitable distribution of resources across various initiatives remains an ongoing challenge. This entails assessing the specific needs of different partners and initiatives within the movement. A fair and inclusive approach is essential to prevent resource imbalances, ensuring that every facet of the initiative receives the support required for its success. Transparency and cooperation among partners are key to achieving this balance, and continuous vigilance is necessary to monitor and adjust resource allocation as needed.

**Recognizing Diversity of Experiences** Mental health experiences and expressions vary across cultures and communities. Recognizing these variations are important to the success of the Mental Health Awareness Revolution. The movement's approach must be adaptable, respecting cultural nuances and ensuring that the principles of empathy and understanding are universally embraced. This includes tailoring initiatives to different cultural contexts, providing materials in various languages, and promoting culturally sensitive approaches to mental health conversations. The importance of culturally competent mental health support cannot be overstated, and the movement continually seeks to adapt to different cultural perspectives while promoting a universal message of empathy and support.

## Hypothetical Scenarios Conclusion

The Mental Health Awareness Revolution underscores the incredible potential inherent in the integration of social moments, partnerships, and empathy. This continuous initiative transforms mental health awareness from a one-time event into a multi-touch program. The power of empathy-driven partnerships emerges as communities, organizations, and individuals work in tandem to improve mental health support, break down stigma, and inspire lasting change. Although challenges persist, the movement's adaptability and unwavering commitment to empathy-driven principles emphasize the vital role such an approach plays in addressing complex and deeply ingrained societal issues. By continuing to create social moments resonating with stakeholders and promoting empathy, we can build a future where mental health receives the attention, resources, and compassion it deserves.

This use case, alongside the Global Clean Water Initiative and the Education Equality Movement, demonstrates that empathy, collaboration, and meaningful moments can mold a more compassionate world. It reinforces the notion that social moments are not sporadic occurrences but are movements for lasting change. These moments hold the potential to transform mental health awareness from a struggle into a global revolution of support, understanding, and healing.

As we continue to address the complex social challenges of our times, it's imperative that we recognize and harness the collective strength of the SPH model. By doing so, we can inspire individuals and organizations to work collaboratively, with empathy as the driving force, toward a more equitable and compassionate world. The Global Clean Water Initiative, the Education Equality Movement, and the Mental Health Awareness Revolution have demonstrated their potential to create transformative change. The stories of water accessibility, education equality, and mental health awareness serve as compelling examples of how empathy-driven initiatives can make a profound difference in the lives of individuals and communities.

The challenges of sustainability, resource allocation, cultural sensitivity, and innovation are real, but they are not insurmountable. These challenges are part of the ongoing journey of social impact, requiring adaptability, creativity, and a commitment to the values of empathy and collaboration.

Ultimately, the power of social moments lies in their ability to bring people together, not just for a fleeting moment, but for a lasting impact. They serve as a starting point for partnerships and empathy-driven change to grow and thrive. By continuing to weave these threads together, we can create an opportunity for social transformation that is inclusive, powerful, and enduring. The future of social impact is bright when empathy, collaboration, and meaningful moments unite to make the world a better place.

CHAPTER

# 10

# Final Thoughts

It's never been a better time to be in the impact space, and the future holds tremendous opportunities for the integration of social moments, partnerships, and the human element as core components of social impact initiatives. As we look ahead, it becomes increasingly clear that the synergy of these elements is vital in addressing complex challenges and driving positive change. Here is where this integration can lead and why it is essential to focus on these concepts now.

## The Imperative of Integration

The need to integrate social moments, partnerships, and the human element is more evident than ever. Traditional approaches to addressing societal challenges are proving inadequate in the face of the growing complexity and interconnectivity of global problems. To tackle modern issues, from environmental crises like climate change to persistent economic disparities and unforeseen public health emergencies, a new framework is needed.

The integration of the three pillars of the SPH model is no longer optional but vital. The synergy of social moments, partnerships, and the human element offers a comprehensive framework that enables us to address the nuances of modern global issues. It provides a platform for inclusive, collective responses that are capable of addressing not only the symptoms but the root causes of these complex challenges. It emphasizes that, at the heart of social impact, there are people with shared stories, aspirations, and the determination to create a better future for all.

## The Changing Landscape of Social Impact

We are in a state of constant transformation, with the pandemic massively accelerating that transformation. Social impact initiatives have moved beyond mere charity and philanthropy, emphasizing sustainability, inclusivity, and scalability. These initiatives are no longer exclusive to nonprofit organizations; businesses, governments, and individuals are recognizing their roles in driving social change. That is why now is the time to deploy this new framework, which can address these multifaceted problems effectively.

The combination of social moments, partnerships, and the human element offers a compelling vision for the future. We're in a time that feels overly complex, interconnected, and rapidly changing. These concepts are essential in creating effective and long-lasting solutions. The integration of social moments provides a platform for shared experiences and mobilization. Partnerships enable collaboration, resource sharing, and the scaling of initiatives. Empathy forms the core of a human-centered approach, fostering understanding, compassion, and collective action.

As we look to the future, these concepts will continue to evolve and adapt to the changing landscape of social impact. They will empower individuals, organizations, and communities to tackle systemic issues, respond to crises, and address global challenges. The time is now to recognize the collective strength of social moments, partnerships, and empathy and harness it to inspire a more equitable and compassionate world. By doing so, we will build a path forward that is grounded in shared purpose and human connection, and that truly leaves no one behind in the pursuit of a better future.

# Index